Praise for Enlightened Parenting

"Every parent hopes to be a wise, loving, and supportive presence in the lives of their children. And, thankfully, every one of Meryl Davids Landau's beautiful essays sheds light on the concerns, challenges, and doubts we all face along the way. The valuable lessons Meryl shares will no doubt help readers develop their own unique, gratifying, and mindful parenting practice."
—**Priscilla Warner, bestselling author of *Learning to Breathe* and co-author of *The Faith Club***

"This delightful collection of essays encourages us to celebrate the lives of our children and our role as their guide, their student, and their companion. Meryl Davids Landau helps awaken us to our authentic selves and thus cultivate that quality in our children."
—**Louise Goldberg, bestselling author of *Classroom Yoga Breaks* and *Yoga Therapy for Children with Autism and Special Needs***

"*Enlightened Parenting* is an insightful and soulful collection of essays on how to parent centered in our heart. Meryl Davids Landau includes practical suggestions for bringing spirituality into the busy daily family life most of us lead, and for nurturing our own spirituality as parents, so that we can model and inspire our children by example. Her down-to-earth approach, including many anecdotes from her own family life, makes this an engaging read that parents of any faith will appreciate."
—**Lisa Erickson, blogger at Mommy Mystic**

"Reading *Enlightened Parenting* feels like you're being embraced by a loving sister who's been there and is helping you along your own mindful parenting journey."
—**Susan Caruso, director, Sunflower Creative Arts for children**

Praise for Meryl Davids Landau's novel,
Downward Dog, Upward Fog

"Lorna's soul journey is the topic of Meryl Davids Landau's first novel, an inspirational gem that will appeal to introspective, evolving women…. Through Lorna, Landau plays out—in a light, easily digestible narrative—the tension between the discipline and insights of spiritual practice on one hand, and embracing the slings and arrows of living in the present."
—Foreword Reviews

"A lighthearted novel about a woman who just can't seem to stay on the spiritual path, something most of us can relate to."
—Yoga Journal Buzz Blog

"Women who loved *Eat, Pray, Love* have been hoping for another page-turner that reflects their spiritual goals… Meryl Davids Landau fills the void."
—Natural Awakenings magazine

"As Lorna Crawford discerns what elements should be added or removed from her life, she meets the very familiar and typical challenges all people face when embarking on a spiritual journey. Complete with the test of personal tragedy, this book will meet you with the truth that yoga or spiritual practices like meditation have more to do with how we meet life's challenges rather than how well we hold an asana or how many thoughts we have while sitting on our meditation cushion."
—Spirituality & Health Books in Bloom newsletter

"*Downward Dog, Upward Fog* is sure to delight spiritually evolving women…. Told with humor and sensitivity, Lorna's struggles are sure

to resonate with anyone on the path of conscious awareness."
—**Science of Mind national newsletter**

"How delicious to find a novel for women who find spirituality every bit as enticing as fashion. The characters in Meryl Davids Landau's page-turner aren't the only ones uplifted—the reader gets a dose of inspiration along with a mesmerizing story."
—**Victoria Moran, bestselling author of *Creating a Charmed Life***

Enlightened Parenting

A Mom Reflects on Living
Spiritually With Kids

Meryl Davids Landau

ap Alignment
Publishing
company

Boca Raton, Florida

ISBN 978-1-936586-22-6

Book design by Teddi Black
Ebook design by Meg Silver

Visit the author's website at MerylDavidsLandau.com
Twitter @MerylDL
Facebook Meryl Davids Landau

Printed in the United States of America

For my loving husband Gary,
my wonderful parents and sisters, and
my beautiful kids—who all made me the mother I am.

Contents

Say No Sometimes
Carve Out a Sacred Space
Call an Old Friend
Expose Yourself to Positive Images
Follow Your Passions
Create!

Introduction

Your newborn baby enters this world. You touch his tender skin, gaze into his eyes, inhale those sweet smells, and know that an angel has come to be with you.

Fast forward 3, 6, or even 17 years. That same child is throwing blocks at your head—or worse, insults at your character. He scribbles on your wallpaper or scratches your new car. It doesn't matter if you spend 23 hours of your day waiting on him, he resents the time you cater to others (or to yourself). When you gaze at that child now, it can be harder to know that he is that angel, and to overflow with that same unconditional love.

This issue was hot on my mind more than 20 years ago, when I became pregnant for the first time. I had seen friends enamored with their infant, clear that their child is the embodiment of love and spirit. Yet, somehow, years later, those same parents became angry, alienated from, or disappointed in their kids.

This upsetting notion took on greater focus in the second trimester of my first pregnancy, when I ran into an old college friend. Or, rather, when she ran into me—literally. Terri was charging down the sidewalk in our town's center, wildly pushing her 4-year-old son in his stroller. As the boy screamed, tears streaming down his face, his mother yelled a hurtful comment intended to silence him. The look on her face as she did so was light years from love. Then she shoved the stroller so hard she accidentally clipped my leg as I coincidentally wandered by.

The last time I had seen Terri, her son was just a few months old. I had joined her on a park bench; she was glowing as she held her priceless treasure. I have no idea what the child did to upset her those four years later. But as I looked down with adoration at my own growing abdomen, at the spiritual being I had taken to calling "my beloved passenger," I was horrified by how disconnected Terri had become. I vowed that this wouldn't happen to me. That I would work hard to maintain the link between my highest, most-loving self and that of my children, no matter how they might behave.

For years before that first pregnancy, staying on my spiritual path had been my daily priority. I meditated twice a day (well, most days); taught yoga; read spiritual literature of myriad stripes; studied with swamis, rabbis, reverends, and other enlightened people; and attended numerous workshops, retreats, study groups, and lectures. I had reached the point where I was largely able to see the divinity inside others—or at least to be aware of when I was falling short.

When I got pregnant, I knew that parenting would challenge my spirituality as never before. Even before my son's birth, I understood that my future children would sometimes lose their own connection to what—with a nod to spiritual author Esther Hicks—I call Source or Higher Self (and others call Spirit, God, Nature, the Universe…). They'd no doubt have tantrums and meltdowns, treat other people poorly, and make choices that would contradict my desires—as I did with my own parents!—all actions that could readily provoke less-than-lofty responses from me.

My children have now been in my life for more than two decades, and I can say with confidence that I was right: they have done those things, and I have done those things. But I can also say that, while I haven't always succeeded in my goal of constantly parenting from an enlightened space (a wholly unrealistic aspiration for anyone, I can see in hindsight), my track record wasn't terrible. When I look at my children today, I do still see the spiritual beings I glimpsed when each first appeared as a babe in my arms.

I have come to believe that any parent can commit him- or herself to the goal of enlightened parenting, to see Source's light emanating from their child even when that child's behavior mutes—or completely obscures—that light. That's because an enlightened perspective is never about changing other people's actions, at least not directly. When my young son teased his sister or my daughter screamed in public at the top of her lungs, I could choose to join their negativity and drag us all even further from our highest selves (which I freely admit I did on occasion), or I could shine understanding and love on the situation to keep myself connected, and perhaps, as a side benefit, elevate us all.

Of course, I did not come to this place of parental wisdom by myself; I had major assistance. First and primarily, I have the daily help of Source. Anytime I ask for guidance, sitting still for even a few minutes to hear the answer, I have not been disappointed. Second, I've had my wonderful husband; my own parents; several amazing early-childhood, preschool, and elementary-school teachers my kids (and I) were fortunate to know; and some loving friends. Third, I met several parents soon after my first child was born who were grappling with similar questions as I was; together we formed a spiritual parenting group (whose members changed over time), to chew over these issues. Many of the suggestions I have sprinkled throughout this book sprang from these discussions.

Finally, and most significantly, I was blessed to come across spiritual writings that inspired me over the years—most not specifically about parenting, but whose lessons I could easily apply. These included Neale Donald Walsch's *Conversations With God* books, Esther Hicks' "Abraham" work, the late Wayne Dyer's teachings, Jon Kabat-Zinn's mindfulness materials, Swami Satchidananda's and Swami Jyotirmayananda's writings, and everything Eckhart Tolle has produced. In studying these materials, certain truisms jumped out as the perfect answers to questions I'd been pondering about what kind of parent I could choose to be. Over the years—most especially when my children were very young—I took some of my reflections and began composing the essays that make up this book, both for the purpose of clarifying my own thoughts and, later (when I had a broader perspective), for sharing them with others who are deep in the experience of raising kids. That time is now.

Notice I said the "experience" of raising kids. Not the "task" of raising them or the "job" of it. Although it may feel like that sometimes, especially when we feel disconnected from Source, children are not a burden. As author Cheryl Strayed writes in *Tiny Beautiful Things*, "children are giant endless suck machines.... They take everything.... [But they] also give you everything back. Not just all they take, but many of the things you lost before they came along." The act of caring for your child—completely overwhelming in the early years, I'm sure we all agree—isn't even a hindrance to your own spiritual growth. When we approach parenting as a sacred calling, it becomes the perfect path to personal enlightenment.

The unconditional love that is the essence of Source is most easily experienced when we hold our newborn child. If we remain open to this state as our child grows, we can eventually enlarge the envelope and bring that same love to others we encounter. That is a good thing, because what parent has time to attend all those retreats, teach (or even do much) yoga, or sit for long daily meditations, as I did before my kids were born? Parenting is a great spiritual practice because it forces us to open ourselves to our higher essence right where we are.

One of my favorite quotes comes from my earliest spiritual teacher—after my grandmother—Swami Satchidananda (the swami who opened the Woodstock festival in the 1960s with the chanting of "Om"). The late founder and director of the Integral Yoga Institute in New York (where I once taught yoga) used to say that parents who bathe, feed, and dress their young "living gods" are doing more for their spiritual growth than if they headed to the mountaintop to meditate. As Satchidananda deliciously put it, "If you ignore your children and go sit and close your eyes, then God says, 'What is this? You offer a piece of fruit on the altar, but I am here in your home in the form of your child and you ignore me.'"

This is the essence of enlightened parenting. The term does not mean imparting spiritual values to your children, although that may result. Rather, it is the every-moment practice of calling upon your highest self when you interact with your child, regardless of whether he is planting a luscious kiss on your lips or calling you a nasty name. It is remaining mindful of your own personal limitations and growing beyond them as you respond to your kids. And it means not judging your child (or, crucially, not judging yourself), giving her the space to create her life the way she chooses, knowing that every creation is absolutely perfect.

I have organized the book into three sections: *Attitudes, Actions,* and *Nourish Yourself.* Knowing that parents have limited time (there were years when my kids were babies that I read only magazine articles rather than books), I have kept each essay short and self-contained. In the first section, *Attitudes,* I reflect on the shifts in heart and mind that dramatically alter our parenting. In the second, *Actions,* I offer concrete suggestions for experiences, rituals, and tweaks in your family and home life that you may want to experiment with. (If any don't speak to you, ignore them; it's important that you be guided by your own inner voice.) Finally, *Nourish Yourself* is a testament to my belief that we can give our children only what we have within us. I most assuredly do not advocate abandoning young children to go off on adventures that gratify our ego. But I have come to see that all parents must dip their quill in the spiritual inkwell for at least a few moments each day if they hope to continually parent in a conscious way. Since many other books deal with general practices for personal spiritual growth, I have limited myself to those specifically useful for time-pressed moms and dads with little ones underfoot.

I've always believed that real-world examples and personal sharing (including of my own fallibilities) speak louder than pronouncements from the mountaintop. Not being on the mountaintop, I can't pronounce from there anyway. (Readers of my spiritual women's novel, *Downward Dog, Upward Fog,* know that there is much of me in Lorna, the protagonist on her own uneven spiritual journey.) I am not a guru, nor a child-development expert; I'm merely a fellow parent working things out as I go along. Many of the essays that follow include intimate stories from myself and from other parents who have been gracious enough to share them with me. To protect privacy, I have changed the names of most of the participants and made a few others into composite characters. I have also alternated between "him" and "her" in describing a child, so as not to always lean on the gender-biased, if grammatically correct, male pronoun.

Whenever your day gets particularly hairy—and how can it not, when it includes tending to children's needs, running a house, nurturing other relationships, nourishing yourself, and possibly also paying work—consider this quote, which has long hung on my wall, from Neale Donald Walsch's *Conversations With God, Book 1*: "Live in your God space and the events become blessings, one and all."

Here's to the blessings your child is bringing you. The essays that follow are intended to help you remember that every day.

Attitudes

"To change our lives,
we need only change our minds."
—Gerald Jampolsky, M.D.

Attitudes

What Kind of Parent Do You Choose to Be?

Two days after delivering my first child in a New York City hospital, the doctor told me my baby was too jaundiced to be discharged. "You go home and rest tonight, and come back to be with him tomorrow," a nurse soothed me. "We'll take special care of your child." Swayed by the authority of the medical establishment (and a desperate need for sleep), I nervously obliged.

When I returned early the next morning, I found my precious bundle screaming his lungs out in the nursery bassinette. A nurse sat nearby, feeding another baby, ignoring my newborn's obvious distress. As I rushed to pick up and coddle my child, the nurse exclaimed, "It's a tough world out there, and he might as well learn that early."

In all the years since I became a mother, I am probably the most grateful to that woman in the nursery. Right there, so early in my mothering, she taught me the most precious lesson of all: All the parenting advice in the world has nothing whatsoever to do with my child and me. (She also taught me that I'd rather not repeat that experience, freeing me to birth my second baby at home.) That woman may believe it's important to toughen up her little charges, but my choice is to be someone who nurtures and protects them.

Who am I as a parent? I saw clearly in that hospital nursery that I am someone who aims to come from love; who tries to view my children's experiences through their own eyes; who knows that my son and daughter are spirits creating a physical experience (as I am), not clay for me to manipulate or mold. Sure, in the frenzy of a moment, I may not remember my self-definition or act from that place, but that is the vision I strive for.

I realized years ago that it is not a character flaw to decide that you want to be a different kind of parent today than you were yesterday—or even than you had chosen to be for all of your years of parenting until now. I'm not talking about changing willy-nilly, but instead giving yourself permission to evolve and grow. This may mean that yesterday you told your son that he could not play a shrieking and running game in the living room, but today as you decide you want to cherish joy, you not only allow the game, you encourage it. (Of course, you can choose to leave the room or stuff cotton in your ears.) Or it may mean that yesterday you sent your child to her room with a stern word when she threw her dinner on the floor, but tonight when she repeated that action you simply explained why wasting nature's bounty makes your heart sad. A change doesn't mean you were wrong yesterday; rather, that now you are consciously coming from a higher perspective.

I remember once taking my daughter to an indoor playground for the afternoon. While we romped, we watched a mom drag her little girl into the bathroom to literally wash her mouth out with soap, because she had said something unkind. A friend of the woman's, playing the role of angelic guide, cornered the mother on her way out of the bathroom, recounting tales of her own soaped-mouthed childhood, and how it had soured her relationship with her mother. I watched the woman soften as she realized that had been her own story, too, and that she didn't want that for her child. I'm confident this woman chose to react differently the next time her daughter lashed out verbally, even though it was likely hard for her to break the family chain.

Are you the parent you want to be? Do you even know what kind of parent that is? Parents are often surrounded by at least some role models offering visions of whom they *don't* want to be. We see parents who define their child's success according to a narrow (usually materialistic) definition; who withhold love when they don't get what they want from their child; who offer only rules, not possibilities; and who constrict, rather than expand, the child's vision for what her life can become. Maybe you decided early on that you would not be like your own parents, but lacking a different model and the knowledge that the choice truly is yours, you find yourself unconsciously repeating their approaches.

Our society blows potent winds when it comes to the "shoulds" of parenting: Children should be seen but not heard; they should conform to social expectations from the earliest ages; parents should be consistent in their rules and discipline; what other kids do (e.g., use the potty by a certain age, attend formal music or sports classes…) yours should too; children should suppress their natural exuberance except in specific, limited situations; and, my personal favorite, even day-old newborns need to learn the treacheries of the world. It takes heartfelt dedication and not a small amount of courage to steer your boat in a different direction.

The way contemporary society advocates raising children isn't leading many of us where we want to go. As Marianne Williamson writes in her classic, *A Return to Love*, mainstream parenting teaches kids "to think thoughts like competition, struggle, sickness, finite resources, limitation, guilt, bad, death, scarcity and loss." "Love [may be] what we were born with," she observes, "[but] fear is what we have learned here."

Starting today, commit to ignoring any definition of parenting you may have embraced but that no longer suits you, and adopt a more enlightened approach going forward. In other words, resolve, as much as possible, to come from love—from Source—in the daily parenting of your precious child.

Attitudes

Love Without Strings

Years ago, Michael Kennedy, a nephew of the late President John
F. Kennedy, died while playing football on skis. Many categorized
his death as just the last in a series of stupid choices he made in
his life. But not his mother. She seemed to have supported every
action Michael took. Sometimes that support was shared by many,
such as when he started a low-income energy company. But other
times, mom stood by him alone, like when he was caught reportedly
sleeping with his children's teenage babysitter and his wife threw
him out of the house. When a disgraced Michael left with no place
to go, it was mom who took him in, giving him not just a home
to stay in but also the uplift that comes from knowing someone
loves you *no matter what you do.*

When I first heard that story, my initial thought was a deroga-
tory, "Only a mother." A second later, however, it hit me in a loving
way: "Only a mother!" (And, likely, a father, too.) The change in
my perception was a "Eureka!" moment for me. I, too, would be
the kind of mother who wraps her arms around her toddler after he

shatters her favorite vase. The kind who might tell her teenager she is beloved not only if she gets A's on her report card, but also if she is truant from school. The kind who embraces her child equally when others praise him and when his misdeeds earn their disapproval. The kind, like Michael Kennedy's mother, who supports and adores her children, little or grown, without conditions or strings. Who constantly asks herself how Source views each parenting situation, and tries to climb to a similar vantage.

This is not to say that enlightened parents don't provide guidance to help a child understand when his actions hurt himself or others (see "Discipline From Your Heart"). It simply means letting your child know that, regardless of what he does, you will always be open to him, trying to look past any negative actions to see, and bless, the higher self within him.

I find this easiest to do when I create a mental picture of my newborn child: my son first placed in my arms in the hospital, my daughter nursing soon after her birth at home. It didn't matter that my son had jaundice or that his hair spiked up straighter than a platoon of soldiers, or that my daughter's skin was wrinkly and red. To my husband and me, they were the most beautiful, sacred, and perfect creations. Over the years, when my kids did things that got my back up, I conjured that image, reminding myself that they are still the same beings as those blessed babies.

I know a person who taught yoga classes to young men in jail, and another who regularly visited (candy in hand) truants in detention centers. What each of them told me when I asked why they did that is that everyone needs to feel that someone can see past their mistakes to acknowledge and bless the perfect spirit inside them. All of us can attest to the fact that when someone puts their faith in us, even when we feel we don't "deserve" it, we're more likely to rise to the occasion and become worthy of that support. And, indeed, that is what happened with many of the troubled people whom these volunteers encountered.

Loving unconditionally, no matter what our child does, is not easy. We're used to people placing conditions on their affection, which is why so many were flabbergasted when the late Saint John Paul II expressed his love for the man who tried to kill him. But we don't have to be a saint to glorify our child. Your parents may have displayed their love only when you did the "proper" thing—when you made them proud or at least didn't cause any major embarrassments—and maybe you've fallen into the trap of withholding expressions of your love when the occasion seems to warrant. But being that steady star always available to your child is what will help her ultimately get back on track when she does falter. You want your child to feel comfortable telling you when she gets in trouble in school, rather than being the kid who keeps her terrible secrets tight. And when teens run away and find life on the street unbearable, it's the ones who know their parents will lovingly open their arms if they return who have a shot at redemption.

Every child needs to know that somebody can see her higher spirit no matter how lowly she acts on a given day. That she is loved simply because she exists, not because of what she does. For your child, vow that that somebody will be you.

Attitudes

Be a Sherpa, Not a Shepherd

What is my role as a parent? To be a guide? A guard? A goaltender? I found myself struggling with these questions when my son was five—old enough, I felt, to know what was expected of him—yet he just wouldn't go with the flow. When other kids sat listening to the preschool teacher read a story, he could be found in the sandbox or block corner creating worlds of his own. (Fortunately, his child-centric preschool let him do that.) At his young friends' birthday parties, he could never be coaxed to pin the tail on the donkey or to pass the parcel. And when his younger sister and I danced around the living room to a rousing samba, he sat on the couch, unwilling to jump in.

Was I supposed to file down his squared edges to help him fit into the circle of life, I wondered; should I strive to help him see the virtues of going along? Is my role to herd him along the path that I determine, from a perspective of wisdom and experience, makes for an easier life?

Eventually, I came to realize that the answers were no. My job as a parent is to water the seed, ensure it gets sufficient sunlight, and watch my child's desires unfold into whatever flower he decides to be. It doesn't matter if I adore marigolds, or if roses get the most lavish social approval. What matters is that my child may prefer to be a daffodil. My role is to help him be the most magnificent daffodil possible, which in his case involves contemplation over commotion.

In their book *Spiritual Parenting,* ministers Gayle and Hugh Prather liken a parent's job to that of an Asian Sherpa. Though the Sherpa intimately knows the route, he does not lead the climber who has come to scale the mountain. He assists, encourages, and supports; never orders, belittles, or takes the starring role. If the climber chooses to retreat, the Sherpa turns back with him. And when the climber is close to reaching the peak, the Sherpa ensures that the climber remains the focus. Your child, too, must summit his own life as he wants it to be, something that will likely be done without much acknowledgment of your assistance, patience, and love.

(Enlightened parents might also realize that, from a spiritual perspective, kids are closer to Source than we are. They don't do as much thinking and planning as adults, so they are more prone to living in the moment, where the most authentic and inspired choices are made.)

I often see parents, myself included, fall into the pattern of wanting to steer our child towards the social goodies we didn't get for ourselves. Clumsy parents might push their daughter into weekly gymnastics classes, even though she prefers to be home reading. Those denied musical education might enroll their kid in trumpet lessons; but what if he'd rather experience music by streaming rock or rap on his phone? Parents need to step back to see how our child's desires differ from our own—how she might choose to live her life absent a parental agenda, however well-meaning ours might be.

A father at a spiritual parenting discussion group I regularly attended talked about wanting his young son "to go into a profession like medicine, law, or accounting, so he wouldn't have to struggle financially like I have." This sentiment is widespread, and it's understandable. But other parents in the group shared how they'd felt pressured by their own parents to similarly "do something practical," instead of pursuing their beloved art, music, or philosophy, to their lifelong regret. In my own circle of acquaintances, there's a doctor who was so depressed by having been pushed into medicine when he wanted to be an airline pilot that he eventually turned to alcohol to numb the disappointment; another waited until his forties to abandon his long-hated career in the family business to study cooking in Paris.

The enlightened approach—and the one that would lead to better odds for lifelong joy—is to nourish a child's own aspirations, whatever they might be. Maybe your child will choose a practical and well-paying career in computer engineering, as my son has, or maybe he'd rather eschew financial gain and help needy people around the world, as my daughter prefers. When the mother of a man I know, who has spent his adult life working and studying at an ashram, finally made peace with his decision, both of them were the happier for it.

Careers aren't the only area where parental expectations can crush a child's dreams. A friend remembers as a child experiencing intense joy while singing, until the day her father admonished her not to croon so loudly since she "couldn't carry a tune." She never uttered a note again, leaving the singing to her more "talented" sister. How sad.

I literally applauded when, during his acceptance speech at the 2016 Tony Awards, actor and rapper Daveed Diggs recalled a moment from his preschool days. Diggs (who played both Thomas Jefferson and the Marquis de Lafayette in *Hamilton*) said all the kids were supposed to participate in a program for the parents, but Diggs demurred. His mother agreed that he could opt out, so instead he and his father—both donning rainbow tights—performed a gymnastics routine. Diggs traced his mother's giving him "permission to do something nobody else was doing" and his father's "supporting me and making it possible" with setting him on the unique trajectory that led to that award.

Be honest about any agenda you are trying to push onto your child and come to terms with letting it go. Your child has her own dreams to pursue, her own life to chart and to live. Of course, this freedom doesn't diminish the importance of your role, which is to watch and listen closely to uncover her chosen path, and encourage (i.e., give courage to) her to explore what she is drawn to (within the bounds of safety, of course). It's also appropriate to voice your opinions when you feel strongly.

But, like that Sherpa, you must then step back and applaud whatever choices your child ultimately makes. Even if you don't agree, and even if you think that, being older and wiser, your views should count for more, allow her to set her own direction. Your child may be a chip off the old block, but it is the job of an enlightened parent to ensure that the chip is whittled into a work of art of the child's own making.

Attitudes

Have Faith, Not Fear

Fear may be a four-letter word, but it is one all parents fall victim to at least some of the time. It's the emotion lying just beneath the warm love inside our heart. Is my child keeping up academically with his peers? Will my "lax" discipline result in an unsocializable outcast? Will my toddler ever let me pee alone? Will my little girl run into the street when I am momentarily distracted? Will my teenager feel the pull of drugs? Will my sweet child hate me some day?

In today's "worst case scenario" society, it is easy to give in to the pull of fear, reacting as if worst case will become inevitable case. But as most spiritual teachings emphasize, fear is the polar opposite of love—when you're feeling one, you're blocked from the other. Whether we are aware of it or not, in every moment we have the option of choosing which it will be.

I remember the first time I saw a parent consciously choose fear in an effort to control her child. I was a new mom taking a stroll with my baby in a nearby mall (in the sizzling summer it's a great place to walk). A frazzled mother was trying to get her 2 year old off the mechanical horse ride, no doubt so she could accomplish at least one errand in the mall that day. "If you don't come with me, that scary monster around the corner is going to grab you," she told her child.

I was horrified watching what I am convinced is a life-scarring, if temporarily effective, tactic. But I have since accepted the reality that all parents—myself included—sometimes resort to one "scary monster" or another to get our way. Our monsters might not be as direct or as extreme, but they can unnerve our child just the same.

One of the most common monsters is to imply that we will love our child less if she doesn't do what we desire. We don't have to say those words, but our child picks up on it all the same. In those moments, we not only deprive her of her connection to Source—which is, after all, pure love—we deprive ourselves of it, too. Another is to threaten to keep our child from her favorite activity or possession.

I find it helps when faced with the choice of love or fear to remember a time in my parenting when I was sure Source was guiding me, and to remind myself that this is always the case. One of those moments occurred early in my pregnancy, when I was working as a magazine editor in a newsroom jammed with dozens of desks topped with large computers. My desk was near the back of four other computers, and since I knew that most radiation from these older models escaped from that side, I worried about keeping my desk where it was. But I hadn't yet told my office that I was expecting, in case the pregnancy didn't take. I was sitting at my desk on a Monday morning, silently scheming how I could switch to a less exposed spot, when my boss came over and announced that our department was moving. To a more isolated corner. That very day.

The "coincidence" was overwhelming, and I put that word in quotes because I'm certain that my pure desire tapped me into the power of Source, which can move mountains if we stay out of the way.

Those same "coincidences" reaffirming my faith happened continuously as my children grew: my firstborn made his entrance a month before his due date, late enough to be perfectly healthy but early enough to give me an extra month's paid maternity leave at home. And when I wondered how that same child would fare in elementary school, since he had such a strong independent streak, I "happened" upon a neighbor who was driving her son 18 miles to a private Montessori grammar school; we soon signed him up. That school proved so fabulous we later sent our daughter there, too. I also "accidentally" discovered a group of people involved in the "cohousing" movement (see "Create Community"), and while to my disappointment we never got one up and running, what I learned from the experience helped me facilitate the close-knit neighborhood we now have.

Of course, it's not practical to think you will never feel fear about your child. My daughter clung to me like Saran wrap for several years, causing me to fret that she'd never learn to be independent. (Turns out she has a horrible sense of direction and was sticking to me to keep herself from getting lost. Needless to say, she eventually let go.) My son almost failed the eighth grade, because he mentally shut down and stopped doing his work midway through the year, worrying me that he would be a middle-school dropout. (He's now getting his master's degree in computer science from an elite university.)

Fear is an emotion I believe deserves only a minuscule place in our mind. If our preteen asks to spend the evening in a dangerous part of town, we might legitimately worry and say no. But when our preschooler needs to spend night after night cuddled in our bed, our third-grader no longer wants to go to grandma's for the weekend (triggering our fear that grandma will be furious), or our kid fails an "important" test, we must open our heart to love.

Peggy O'Mara, the founding editor of the nurturing magazine *Mothering*, believes that this is the heart of parenting. "There is really only one decision that underlies all other decisions concerning our children," she once wrote in an editorial. "This decision is whether we will choose love or fear; whether we will accept or resist the situations that happen with our children; whether we will choose to cooperate or to be adversarial with our children."

In other words, whether we can look even the most unsettling situation in the eye, and not summon the monster around the bend.

Attitudes

Don't Try to Just Get By

How often do you find you're playing with your child but your mind isn't with you? For most of us, staying present is a rare event.

I know how difficult it can be to remain as mindful as our child: when my son was in preschool, he could launch and repair, launch and repair, launch and repair his battery-powered rocket all afternoon; I lost focus by the second blast-off. The fifth time around a Monopoly Jr. board could always find me mentally wandering to my actual real estate holdings rather than those in the game. And don't even get me started about Dr. Seuss' *The Foot Book*; when my young daughter whipped out that ditty for the thousandth time, I could barely keep my own feet from racing from the room, so naturally I read it with my thoughts elsewhere.

Mindfulness is a crucial spiritual (and stress-reduction) practice. But even more importantly for parents, when you align with your child in any moment, you let her know that she matters more than anything else. As you do in the company of your reverend, rabbi, priest, or guru, he deserves nothing less than to be graced by your complete presence.

This doesn't mean that you must focus on your child all the time; that isn't healthy for either of you. When you really are too busy or too bored with your child's activity, there's no shame in admitting this. It can even be beneficial. As a mom I know frequently observes, sometimes kids need the "benign neglect" of their parents to really get a creative project going. But once we agree to be in his world, we must do so in a way that communicates that he merits our full presence.

Where does your mind go when you let it wander when you're with your child? Mine slips to work left on my computer undone, bills to pay, chores I haven't finished, or grocery items on my list. But when I step back and ask myself if any of these is more important than my child, the obvious answer is no.

We may think we are "getting by" when we split our attention, but our child inevitably notices. That's because total attention lights up the person we are focused upon. A singular focus elevates our mind, causing us to connect with our higher self. The person we focus on senses that energy and love emanating from us.

People who met Bill Clinton when he was president often said they were amazed by how intently he put his attention on them. He felt their pain, embraced their joy, understood their needs. (Being a politician, however, he didn't always act in ways they might have expected from their conversation.) People adored that attribute of Clinton's because it is so rare. And if it is rare for adults to fully focus on one another, it is all that much rarer for grownups to do it with kids.

Mindfulness is a muscle that must be practiced—but once you

master it, you can bring that ability to every moment in your life. The spiritual exercises of deep breathing, meditation, maintaining silence, and performing sacred service are all ways to train the mind to fix on the current situation. (See essays on those topics in the *Actions* section.)

Often, we think we're being more mindful than we are. I remember as a teenager telling my parents I could easily do my homework with the TV blaring. Since my grades were good, they let me do it. I learned the material just enough to spit it back out on a test, but in retrospect I didn't focus deeply enough to really learn it. What's more, I was training my mind to embrace diversions. For years, I would be in the most breathtaking mountain or beachfront trail and find that my thoughts had raced away. One late afternoon, while sitting on the beach on the west coast of Florida, my mind was so distracted by a work problem that I didn't even notice the sun magnificently drop into the ocean. It took years of practice to be able to "be here now," as the spiritual teacher Ram Das used to say. For the most part, I can now sit down to breakfast by myself and be totally aware of what I'm eating—the texture of the oatmeal in my mouth, the cinnamon exploding on my tongue, the blueberries popping with flavor—without needing to pick up a magazine or flip on the TV and "entertain" my brain.

Meditation masters suggest starting small, by bringing your focus to something you are already doing. The next time you're in the car, for example, turn off the music, don't make idle talk with other passengers, and stay totally attentive to the road ahead. Or keep your mind on your body as you shampoo and soap in the shower, rather than on your plans for the day. Little kids know how to do this naturally—so watch them to learn.

Once you've mastered even a few moments of mindfulness, allow your child's presence to completely fill you as you sit or play with her. You will not only both feel more enlivened, the time will seem to pass more slowly—a boon itself, because your precious years with your young child will flit by fast enough even when you are paying close attention.

⚜

Attitudes

Slow Yourself Down

One Saturday when my children were little, I was leaving the park with them, plus the 6-year-old friend of my son. My hands were full with the remnants of the long day: an emptied picnic cooler, a basket of sandy toys, muddy changes of clothes, and a soggy wind-up boat. I was tired from pushing swings and swinging a toddler; I was desperate to get home.

The children were walking a few yards behind me as we made our way out of the park. My destination—the car, where I could sit!—was finally in view when my daughter discovered an inchworm on the ground. Suddenly, all three kids dive-bombed for a closer look. "No! We have to go," I pleaded, anxiety oozing out my every pore as my mind raced to where I wanted to go: the car, then home.

The pearl of wisdom, a Zen-like reminder of what it's all about, came from my son: "Mom, how often do we see a worm? We want to watch him get off the sidewalk."

Living in the moment. Enjoying the journey. Taking time to survey the moment before you—including those tiny inches beneath your feet. In my haste to get home, I had forgotten this crucial spiritual practice. This important moment in the inchworm's life, and indeed, in ours, was almost missed by my children and by me for the simple reason that I was operating on adult time, not kid time—and adult time says it should take no more than a minute to get from the park bench to the parking lot.

I put down my heavy load and suddenly I realized we had all the time in the world. Who cared if dinner got to the table a little late? If the kids took a shorter bath before bed? It didn't matter where I thought we were supposed to be; where we were was surely the perfect spot for now.

We settled in to watch the worm make its way across the walk. And the most thrilling part is that I don't even know how long we sat there, because I was able to let the moment unfold in its own, magnificent way. Getting lost in the inchworm's life made this final piece in the park the most meaningful of the day.

Just about every parent is in a hurry—getting Emily to school, racing Elizabeth to soccer, lugging Eli to the store—it's no wonder we're frazzled and frayed. But while the world, with its cell phones, 24-hour news cycles, and unending texts and emails, may be spinning ever faster, no law says you must grab hold and constantly race along.

Begin slowing down your life by taking a lesson from your kids: it's okay to divert from your original plans and spend moments in unscheduled endeavors. Instead of wishing that your dawdling children would finally grasp adult time, discover the value of kid time from them. Consider the joy you could have in the morning by spinning an impromptu tale after putting on your child's left shoe but before lacing up her right, or by taking a pause to all breathe in the beautiful begonias on your way out the door.

I remember as a child wondering why I always rushed to get dressed before racing off to grammar school in advance of the bell, yet I had so much leisurely time during our lunch break. It was only later that I realized I could have had a more peaceful morning had I only gotten up a little earlier. Set your own alarm clock a half-hour earlier tomorrow, so you can find that extra space in your day. (If you have to go to bed a little earlier, do so; the energy of the world waking up is so much more magnificent than that of late night, anyway.) Don't pack in extra obligations for the now-longer morning—the idea is to have the time to go with your family's flow, wherever it takes you. If possible, have an unhurried meal; there is nothing like calmly breaking bread with the people you love to nourish your soul.

Pull back on your agenda for the remainder of the day (see "Slash Your Family Must-Do List"). Despite what we all fear, no one suffers from letting go of overscheduled activities. Everyone will instead benefit by being able to enjoy the activity at hand, without worrying about what's coming next.

When cultivating a little slowness, though, be careful not to fall into the habit of sloth. Your family is aiming not to slog through fewer activities with limited energy, but to do everything with a crystal focus and a sense of ease—and with a heart full of love.

Attitudes

Treasure Every Single Day

I was driving home from a breastfeeding support group one evening with my then 3-month-old daughter in the car. She'd just gone from sleeping through the night to getting up every two hours; it was 8 o'clock and I was beat.

A long line of vehicles was stopped in front of me. The guardrails were down at the railroad crossing, the red lights flashing. We waited and waited, but no train came. Then we waited some more. Soon, a few cars tentatively drove around the guardrails; eventually, a steady stream was following their lead, swerving through the obstacles to the other side. I figured what I'm certain they all were thinking, that the signals must be broken.

When I reached the front of the line, I didn't hesitate to begin my own meandering around the rails. But the moment I was dead center on the track, a flash of white light emerged from the darkness: A train was hurtling straight at my baby and me! I slammed on the gas pedal and cleared the track in what seemed like seconds before the steel torpedoed by.

I don't remember pulling off the road or unbuckling her car seat, but the next thing I knew I was in a parking lot, clutching my sleeping infant. I touched her feathery skin, smelled her fruity breath, watched her closed eyes delicately flutter. I embraced her with the unadulterated appreciation I'd had the day she was born, a sensation that until that moment had already diminished—even though she was only 3 months old.

In the years since then, I admit that I haven't always remembered to treat my children as if this were our first and most precious moment together. But it's a goal I strive for to this day.

I know a woman who set herself the challenge of living each day as if it were her last, and I can appreciate the preciousness I would bring to my family interactions if I knew this was going to be my final hurrah. But one's last day would also be tinged with the sadness of loss and the desire to cling to each moment, rather than to let each joyous experience unfold in its own delicate time. Most of us are not as advanced as the man in the spiritual tale who sees tigers at both the top and bottom of the ladder he is climbing, and so decides to consume with gusto the berries he finds on a vine in the middle, knowing that if he can't change his fate he might as well enjoy himself!

I aim for what the Buddhists call "beginner's mind": One filled with heightened observation, rather than the jaded dullness that comes when repeating the same task. A beginner's mind is the approach you had when you changed your baby's diaper those first few days—when you noticed her beautiful skin, cleaned each fold with reverence, and appreciated that a healthy bowel movement meant a healthy baby. Contrast that with the days and months that followed, when your hands moved with the precision of a mechanical factory arm, her bottom simply a part that needed fixing before you went on your way.

It's easy for most parents to bring that "beginner's mind" to our "firsts" with our child—her first solid food, steps, trip to Disney World, discovery of a lizard flitting around the lawn. The challenge is to keep your sense of wonder once those firsts morph into sixths and tenths and fourteen-hundreds. This issue is even more pronounced when we have our second or third (or beyond) child, when it's so easy to feel that we have been there and done that before.

The next time your child comes into the room, stop what you're doing and look at him. Really look. Notice the slight lisp when he speaks, those sparkling eyes that are just like your father's, even his tendency to take an inordinate amount of time to get to the point of his story. Cherish these traits, especially the ones that previously irritated you. They are what make your child all that he is.

One of my favorite life lessons comes from a variety show skit I saw on TV many years ago. As a middle-aged woman and her onscreen husband sit in a restaurant, preparing to meet her younger sister and her sister's new fiancé, the husband rebukes his wife for her grating laugh and her habit of individualizing her food orders. Soon the sister arrives—and it's clear those traits run in the family. Yet the new fiancé finds his partner's laugh and food choices adorable. The contrast between the two men's reactions made for good comedy, but it also reveals a profound truth: The same acts can switch from *treasure* to *turnoff* over time if we allow. Bringing "beginner's mind" to your interactions with your child lessens this impulse.

Treating each day as if it were your family's first also means paying attention to the world around you. When you head for your daughter's soccer game, don't hustle everyone down the street; appreciate the journey as much as your arrival. You needn't be 8 years old to lie on the grass and thrill to the clouds taking shape, or to notice a spider spinning an intricate web on your kitchen window. There's an amazing world around us, but most of the time we adults are oblivious.

My family used to take occasional "listening walks," where we went someplace—even our backyard—and walked in silence. The idea is for everyone to hear what they might otherwise overlook: bird chirps, rustling leaves, a pinecone falling from a nearby tree, even the steady life-affirming breaths of one another. You can take a listening walk in a noisy mall or restaurant; just notice the sounds that are always there, even when we don't pay attention. (Being around a small child helps with this practice: I remember when my son jumped into my arms after a store's intercom system relayed a sale notification—an announcement I wasn't consciously hearing until he reacted.) You can also do a "touching walk," where you luxuriate in textures (including your child's skin, her velvet coat, satin party shoes), or a "watching walk," taking turns to point out what we are generally too distracted to see.

Exercises like these can eventually bring a mindset of wonder and awe to as many moments of as many days as possible. It is a task so difficult even Buddhists who have been practicing for decades struggle, so don't judge yourself harshly if you succeed only once in a great while. Celebrate the fact that that's once more than you likely did before.

Attitudes

Embrace Your Strengths

If you were to describe a position that demands you constantly reach for the highest reaction to even the lowest action, you might choose minister, diplomat, criminal court judge, or even military general. But each of these pales compared to the role of a parent. Parents constantly face situations that force them to either pull condemnation out of one pocket or forgiveness from the other. That test them to blow their cool or tap their inner calm. That demand either paralysis and inaction or courage and strength.

The role of parent requires vast mining of our inner resources. Fortunately, even if we don't know it, we have everything within us to succeed. There's a line in Neale Donald Walsch's *Conversations With God,* attributed to "God," that perfectly describes our fortitude to overcome tough moments with our child: "You are forgiveness and patience, strength and courage.... In moments of your life you have known yourself to be these things. Choose now to know yourself as these things always."

I can chose to know calmness when my child shrieks in the

middle of a crowded store that he must—*must!*—have those new sneakers, even though they are too small for him. (Which he did, and I did). I can tap into my unceasing appreciation for my little daughter, even when I catch her pouring green paint over my new leather shoes. (Ditto, I'm proud to say.)

I once asked a swami what he believed the purpose of relationships to be. The man thought for a full minute before responding: "Rubbing and scrubbing." Being close to another person provides ample opportunities for conflict, he said, and in our responses we can find ways to rise higher and higher. This swami, a celibate monk, was speaking of his relationships with other ashram members—especially a fellow resident with whom he'd had a disagreement that morning (which ended when he decided to drop his objections and give her a loving hug). No relationship offers as much "rubbing and scrubbing" as with your child—a person you intertwine with from her birth, for whom you make astronomical sacrifices, and whose mission, it can sometimes seem, is to discover where all your buttons are located and how best they can be pressed.

There are moments throughout the day, I'd venture, when every parent feels inadequate. It isn't because we are incapable, though; it's because we've disconnect ourselves from knowing our true power.

• *You are capable of total forgiveness.* My friend Robert was feeling alienated from his 3-year-old son, Cody. One night, the boy told Robert he wanted his mother to bathe him, even though this had always been Robert's cherished task. When Robert later found Cody coloring on his work papers, when he had explicitly instructed the boy to stay away, Robert's rage surfaced. He sternly reprimanded Cody, to which the boy, his own shame rising, replied, "I hate you, dad! I hate you!"

You can probably imagine what happened next—except you'd probably be wrong. A wave of forgiveness overtook Robert, so he didn't feel the once-reflective need to fling the hurt right back. "You may hate me," Robert calmly soothed his boy, reaching out to hug him. "But I love you so much."

Forgiveness is a path you can always take—even when you feel you're correct and the other person somehow owes you. It's a quality that will naturally bubble up when you remember that you can be right or you can be happy—and that the latter brings so much more satisfaction.

• *You are capable of endless patience.* My kids went through a phase of digging in whenever we needed to leave the house. "Time to go," I would chirp, heading for the front door, bracing myself for them to act as if I hadn't spoken. "Please give me patience!" I began to implore, looking skyward (years of religious schooling that God is in the heavens was hard to break), agitation rising from my feet to my twitching ears. One day, it dawned on me that I was asking Source as if I needed to be infused with something I didn't already possess.

The next time my kids ignored me, I changed my mantra. "Thank you Source, for giving me an endless supply of patience," I said under my breath. That moment of acceptance provided the space to see my children's perspective: They didn't want to leave because they were having fun. So I told them they could have a few extra minutes but then we really needed to go, and I waited—now genuinely patiently—while they finished. And the most remarkable miracle was that, as I exuded understanding, my kids eventually stopped resisting and got ready on time.

The ability to be calm even when you feel put upon is an ability you know you have: We all would stand calmly in a long line to buy the newest smartphone or cash a prize-winning check at the bank, and you've no doubt kept trying without complaint to connect with an online ticket seller to buy seats to a nearly sold out ballgame or Broadway show. We lose our patience because we think we need to be someplace else, and sometimes we do. But if the cost of racing to our next endeavor is to pinch ourselves off from our higher self, or to create a chink in our relationship with our child, is that worth it? (This may also indicate you've got too much going on: see "Slash Your Family Must-Do List.")

• *You are capable of incredible strength.* A friend once shared a story from her childhood: Her father, overwhelmed by his six kids at home, often spent weekends at his buddy's house or at the bar. When she became an adult, my friend confronted her dad, and he confessed that he did those things because he felt inadequate. "If I regret one thing about my life," he told her that day, "it was allowing other people's vision of me as a weakling to turn me into one. I let that perception cost me years of missed opportunities with you kids."

As author and Native American healer Don Miguel Ruiz observes, each of us comes into adulthood with a distorted image of ourselves, given to us by those around us. Because we have no other mirror, we often embrace that image. But you can correct the funky reflection anytime. Just ponder how often you have demonstrated strength of purpose, character, and will—as far back as your child's first days of life, when you got up numerous times each night to comfort him. If you could handle your screaming infant, you can deal with other challenges parenting throws your way.

• *You are capable of extreme courage.* I never understood the lion character in *The Wizard of Oz.* He says he lacks courage, but he goes off to a foreign place with a group of strangers in search of an unchartered future. If that isn't bravery, I don't know what is. So what if he did it with a quiver in his voice and a shiver in his step? That only means he wasn't in touch with the boldness he was displaying.

Having a child is the ultimate in courageous acts. Like the lion, we leap into an unchartered future. We go through the heroic acts of pregnancy and birth, and we radically alter our life's circumstances the moment our newborn arrives. Why, then, do so many feel as weak-kneed as the lion, especially as our child moves beyond infancy?

I think it's because we live in a culture that revels in fear, that preaches how menacing the world is, and that demands that we all wear armor of protection. In actuality, the world is a marvelous place, full of miracles and wonder—and what it really should demand is that we wear a big smile.

• *You are capable of boundless love.* There's a scene in the *West Wing* where White House staffer Toby Ziegler tells his boss Leo McGarry that he isn't sure he will love his about-to-be-born twins the way a father should, having never had a role model in his own dad. As soon as his kids are born, however, his affection runs so deep he realizes he would even follow a terrorist's command if his babies' lives were ever on the line.

Love isn't like an oil well that dries up when you've tapped it out. It's the rays from the liquid sun, flowing like a waterfall. It doesn't stop because you're tired or your child's having a rough day and making you miserable as a result. Love always resides in the space between you and Source, so when you put your fond attention on your child, Source's love gushes over him, too. You can never dam the love between you and your child; you can only stop seeing that it is there.

The next time you feel overwhelmed by parenting, know that your toolbox is more than stocked for anything that comes your way. As with any good artisan, the ability to use those tools in novel situations is what makes life—and parenting—exciting and fun.

Attitudes

Pass the Pepper With Adoration

My mind and body were tight from a day driving my then-6-year-old son to school and back (18 miles each way), my 2-year-old daughter to an outing at the park, getting writing work in during her nap, taking both to the dentist, finishing that writing assignment, then cooking the family dinner and giving them a bath. I was eager to get the kids to sleep quickly so I could relax, meditate, and have a minute for myself before my lids succumbed to the unyielding force of gravity already trying to tug them down. In other words, a typical evening at home.

But, as was also typical, my son wanted me to help him change his clothes and brush his teeth (even though he was more than capable), then read him several stories and sing him a song. I resisted, but after taking a few deep breaths, I replenished my stock of adoration and was able to accomplish his requests with the gentleness one might use to stroke a butterfly's wings.

The phrase "quality time" is often bandied about in parenting circles, but when most people use it they have in mind a well-planned outing to a museum or an elaborate day trip to the beach. Those special events are indeed wonderful, and become part of the tapestry of memories of your family's life. But like vacations to a beautiful resort or an exciting city, they don't comprise the majority of our lives.

It is clear to me from moments like the one that evening with my son that quality time is any instant when we remember our love and appreciation for our child and allow our words and actions to reflect that. It is quality time when you watch your son twirl in a new dress-up outfit and honor his feelings of excitement and possibilities. It is quality time when you enjoy a piece of beautiful music together. It is quality time when she tells you of a thrilling leaf she found or of an app she played and conquered on the iPad, and you connect with her joyful sense of accomplishment.

Part of elevating a moment's quality is putting yourself in the place of your child. When I used to towel off my young children after their bath, I approached them like I was drying angels who had come to visit (which I believe in a sense they are), rather than mopping up sodden kids about to drip on my floor. When my daughter would tell me about an argument she'd had with a little friend, I'd listen as if this was the most important dilemma in both our lives—because at that moment it was. When I'd have to tell my kids I couldn't take them on a planned outing because a magazine article was taking longer than expected, I'd say the words with the care I'd use if disappointing my boss. And during dinner, when one of them asked me to pass the water pitcher, ketchup, or pepper, I'd hand it over with love. By expressing my unyielding devotion in these little ways, tiny moments were elevated into monumental—indeed, sacred—occasions.

My late Grandma understood that we most clearly touch the face of Source in what seem like the most mundane events in our day. Once, as a teenager, when I stained my favorite shirt before going out with my friends, she took that shirt and scrubbed the stain with vigor—and with love. When Grandma gracefully slipped the clean item over my head a half hour later, it could well have been a silk-and-ermine robe. Similarly, when she'd offer me a piece of the hard candy she always kept in her purse, she did it with such an open heart the bland sweets tasted delicious.

My friend Sheila decided to view each moment as an opportunity to open her heart after her child recovered from a serious bout of pneumonia. While Ben was hooked up to all those machines in the hospital, Sheila constantly beamed her love to the boy. In the first few days after he returned home, she consciously baked her adoration into the foods she made, the stories she read him, the talks they had. But while her heart never wavered, habits and time constraints soon lulled her to her more rote interactions. Sensing the difference in the emotion behind her similar behaviors, one day Ben asked her, "Mom, do you love me more when I am sick?" Sheila realized that it shouldn't take a crisis for her to display the deep affection she always felt. She never took him for granted again.

If you were entrusted with the most precious object in the universe, how would you treat it? Well you *have been* entrusted with such a thing. Although the busyness of our days pull us away from that knowing, strive to recall it the next time you're asked to pass your jewel the pepper.

Attitudes

Cherish All Children, Not Just Your Own

It was the kind of news story that makes you cry. A man had killed his girlfriend's 2-year-old daughter because she dared to eat his sausage from the refrigerator, violently shaking her in a gruesome attempt to get her to throw up the meat. Worse, the TV reporter revealed, the girl's mother stood by and watched, too afraid of her boyfriend to intervene. The man was convicted and jailed. When the judge prepared to sentence the mother, she said something commonly stated: "I would have taken a bullet for my child." Then she added a twist not often heard: "And I would have taken a bullet for yours."

Parents intuitively know that we would endure anything to protect, nurture, and inspire our offspring. It is our role—indeed, our heart's desire—to "take a bullet" for her. But when I heard that judge, I realized that we are not fully open to Source until we know we would protect, nurture, and inspire *all* children, not just our own. People always comment that it takes a village to raise a child; I believe it takes more than that—it takes each and every person on earth.

Most of us don't harm other people's kids—not physically, at least. But I have seen a mother scream at another child in the park because he dared to throw sand at her precious darling. And what parent doesn't know the verbal abuse heaped at children on opposing sports teams? (And even on their own team when a child's actions lead to a loss.) We may think it's fun to razz the pitcher or stare down the basketball center standing between our child and victory, but would you want *your* child on the receiving end of that? Even more, how many of us care enough to try to improve the sub-par schools low-income children go to or the lack of quality foods they can access, as long as our kids are not affected?

I vividly remember being 10 years old and playing volleyball at my day camp's annual "color war" contest. It was the end of the week, so the team with the most cumulative points gleaned from the sports and activities that last day would be crowned champion. Our volleyball game took place when the teams were virtually tied. I had been on the losing side pretty much every year since I started at the camp a few years earlier, so I understood that losing was no big deal. (As an adult, I am amused when people let their day be ruined when "their" professional sports team doesn't win a game.) Most campers didn't share my Zen approach, however; they wanted victory. When the ball soared towards me, I heard the words, "Miss it!" screamed out by a counselor from the opposing team, part of a growing crowd of spectators. I did not. But I was crushed that a person I had long respected wanted me to fail.

Society's notion of "yours" and "mine" has us slotting kids that way, too. How different from African tribesmen who, as Burkina

Faso-born writer Sobonfu Some describes, consider all village members to be family, with kids encouraged to call any adult "mother" or "father."

For years, my children adored a toll collector on the highway we traveled to get to their Montessori school. (This was before widespread electronic passes made collectors largely obsolete.) I always said hello to the woman as I handed her my coins, and she always said it back, beaming. Then she'd turn to my kids in the back seat and greet them. I can still conjure up her "Hiya, kids!" and her broad smile, even though it's been years since I've seen her. It didn't matter if her toll line was longer, my kids always insisted I drive through her lane. Such a simple act of acknowledgment had them glowing the entire morning.

I have always considered myself a "kid person," scooping up my friends' children even before saying hello to my friends; smiling and chatting with strangers' kids at restaurants, parks, or the mall. Yet even I found some children hard to embrace. One nasty girl who lived around my corner was always sneering at people passing by; another, a runny-nosed boy at a local park, used to shove other children (including my own), and sometimes even nip at them with his teeth. Over time, I realized that aiming to see even their inner beauty was a crucial spiritual practice for me. Like all of us, those kids are part of Source. They were just cut off from knowing that, acting out as a cry for loving attention.

I began to speak sweetly to each of them, as if they were my niece and nephew. Rather than tense up when I saw him at the park, I was soon eager to find the boy and chat. I waved and smiled at the girl whenever I passed her. While my intention was not to change their behavior, as you can probably guess each did become nicer—not just to my children but to others as well.

I'm sure there's a "brat" eager for your caress. It's important for our own spiritual growth and for the upliftment of all kids on the planet that we work towards emotionally embracing all children as if they were our own. Even—no, especially—if you encounter him at the playground and he has just taken a bite out of your own little cherub's wings.

📿

Attitudes

Parent Day and Night

Your child cries out for you at 3 PM. He needs you because he's hungry, lonely, hurting, or afraid. If you're like most parents, you don't think twice about comforting him.

Your child cries out for you at 3 AM. He needs you because he's hungry, lonely, hurting, or afraid. If you're like many parents, you're hesitant to comfort him.

Sure, part of the reason is that you're exhausted and need your sleep, so you can parent well or work in the morning. But I believe a key factor hindering parents' embrace of their child in the middle of the night is that our impulse has been questioned by experts who say it is unnecessary, unwise, and even detrimental.

Their rationale is if you coddle your child during the night, you'll create a kid who will need you to do so practically until he leaves for college. Ignore him, some advise, or at most comfort him for a few minutes and then leave.

The first time a mother told me this was the prevailing experts' advice—when my son was a few days old—I was certain she was mistaken. I figured she'd gotten hold of some outdated parenting manual and believed it to be contemporary thinking. After all, isn't this the era where even mainstream physicians recommend breast-feeding into toddlerhood and continuously holding young infants without fear of spoiling? But I soon discovered to my dismay that this was indeed considered state-of-the-art parenting.

What could be wrong with letting a child cry until he finally exhausts himself and goes to sleep? Parents who have done it—who have shut their ears to the shrieking—report that it does work. After three or four nights of screaming with only intermittent comforting, or sometimes three or four weeks, everyone sleeps through the night.

But I believe there's a price to be paid. For one, maybe your baby is in physical pain. A mother once told me she had ignored her daughter's yelps for hours in an effort to "train" her, only to discover the next morning that a hair had been tightly wrapped around the baby's toe, nearly cutting off all circulation. Just because you can't see her feet under her PJs, or the tooth moving under the gum line, or a gassy tummy well before its contents explode into the diaper doesn't mean your child isn't experiencing its discomfort.

Or maybe he's in emotional pain. Our culture doesn't acknowledge psychological woes as much as physical hurts. You're allowed to stay home from school or work because your foot aches, for example, but not because your heart does. But why should feeling scared, lonely, angry, frustrated, or confused be less cause for comforting your child? I know that when I'm sad I want my husband to wrap his arms around me, not shush me and tell me to go back to sleep. Rather than pronounce yourself as your tiny child's rock amidst the shifting emotional sands below all human feet, you proclaim yourself unreliable.

A television reporter once gave an account of her visit to a foreign orphanage. What struck her most, she said, was how silent a building full of babies could be: no cooing, cacophony, and, eerily, no crying. To parents accustomed to endless mayhem, this may at first blush seem blissful. But what could be mistaken as contentment on the part of a placid baby is more likely quiet despair. And I believe that that dejection, albeit on a much milder scale, occurs in the nursery when a parent doesn't arrive in response to a baby's nighttime needs.

It's also bad for our own spiritual growth. If Source is love, can I stay connected when I am behaving in a way that seems cruel? When we ignore our shrieking child, our heart cries out alongside him, which is why most parents have to practically strap themselves to their bed to endure the screaming during the training.

I don't take lightly the need for sleep. I was shocked after my first child arrived to discover that newborns don't actually "sleep like a baby." After living through years of nightly wakings, I understand what can drive a parent to ignore a child in the deep of night. But there are ways of comforting kids that don't result in perpetual bags under your eyes or the punch-drunk exhaustion that can make successfully working or parenting impossible.

My family mitigated our sleep problem by creating a family bed for several years. By bringing in a bassinette, then crib, and finally a twin next to our queen bed and putting up a few guardrails, we happily accommodated everyone's needs. (Some experts point to studies showing the dangers of rolling onto your child, but those almost never account for alcoholism or obesity, and a separate sleeping surface eliminates any risk.) When our child woke up, I barely opened my eyes and still gave him or her the soothing required. I know of other parents who instead placed an extra bed in their nursery, so they could be with their baby when called and still get good sleep. A futon in the corner of the room can also work.

I'm not saying that helping your child learn to fall asleep on her own, especially when she is old enough to understand why her parents need their sleep at night, should never be done. And if you reached your breaking point and already sleep-trained your child, embrace that you did what was best for you at that time. But parents need to go inside and trust their heart more. If you wouldn't do something during the day, why does it become okay simply because it is dark outside?

Despite the experts' prediction, by the way, my kids (and those of other parents I know who heeded their baby's calls) eventually did learn to soothe themselves. No one had to add a crash course in getting to sleep to their child's high school curriculum.

Attitudes

Be Sure Your Limits Are Large

Quick quiz: Which is more important, your connection to your higher self or your child's socks? Inner peace or no crumbs on the floor? Flowing love or racing harried to lessons at the skating rink? I know that in the abstract, I'd choose the former every time. So how come it's so easy to spend much of our day bickering and battling over the latter?

No, you may not wear sneakers without socks. No, you may not eat that cookie away from the table because you'll make a mess. No, we can't go home because I paid for those ice skating lessons and you're going to take them. No to this. No to that. *No, No, No.* In a typical day early on in my mothering, I probably spewed that word at my child dozens of times.

When I realized how often that two-letter message was passing my lips, though, I vowed to turn many of those *No*'s into *Yes*'s.

No's are the constrictors of life, the concept that when heard to excess leads us to fear that every step may lead to trouble, and therefore makes us cautious at every turn.

Yes's are the expanders, the concept that helps us know that we are capable of anything.

I believe that each time a parent says *no* to their offspring, the child diminishes a little bit. I have adult friends who heard *no* throughout much of their own childhood and now won't (literally or metaphorically) color outside the lines. A study published in the *Journal of Creative Behavior*, in fact, found that the most creative schoolchildren came from homes with hardly any rules (although they had plenty of moral guidance), while less creative kids sprang from regimented environments.

Who made all of the rules that we think our child must follow, anyway? Who decided the paths that govern—and limit—all of us? Native American healer Don Miguel Ruiz calls these rules "the dream of the planet." Parents and, later, schools, religious institutions, and governments ensure that each of us adheres to the strictures that developed over time, he observes. But wouldn't our lives, and our world, be so much better if we felt freer to create things the way we want them to be, rather than follow the route someone else determined?

When our babies are small, starting to explore everything they can get their hands (and mouth) on, we consciously reconfigure our homes—putting away treasured glass statues, china, delicate books, and assorted knickknacks—to make them *Yes* environments. As our toddlers age, though, most of us feel comfortable settling into the *No*'s. But knowing what *no* means and liking how it feels are as different as rocks are from rainbows. I'm not referring to the occasional, "I'm sorry I can't do that with you right now," which I think is not only an option but an obligation if we're trying to stay true to our inner selves (see "Say No Sometimes"). I'm talking about a whole dialogue of *no*'s. No, you can't go there. No, you can't touch that. No, you may not eat that now. No, you're wrong about this. No, I can't agree to that. No, that will make too much mess. No, we can't do it the way you want.

I decided to loosen the rules under which my children lived. I made my house a *Yes* environment well past toddlerhood, without fussy furniture or breakable things. (Even when they were teenagers, my son's friends liked to come over because there was so much room to roughhouse.)

I have an artist friend who tells the story of the stark day her childhood *Yes* home became a *No* one. She loved to paint, often doing so in her bedroom. As a byproduct, her carpet was splattered with so many colors that visitors couldn't determine its original shade. When she was 13, she came home to find her carpeting had been replaced without warning. Worse, her parents directed her to keep the new flooring clean. Although she continued to paint in school and art classes, she says she never felt as free with her art again.

Why does any parent feel they must restrain their child? How about: Yes, you can go without socks any day. Yes, you can eat that cookie wherever you want but please try to clean up after yourself. Yes, if you're tired we can skip the skating rink, but if you feel you're doing too much let's cut back next season.

Of course, you can't create a completely rule-free household, nor should you. Some limits are needed for safety (although a much smaller number than we think). Others are necessary for the smooth functioning of a family and a home. A few can even remind us to connect with Source: Former Catholic monk Thomas Moore fondly recalls the rules he lived under in his years at a monastery—strict schedules set aside for meditating, praying, studying, and keeping silent—which served to keep him on his spiritual path.

Sit down with your loved ones and agree on a set of required rules. Keep the list short. Then aim to generate expansive experiences with your *Yes*'s. (Or even *Hell Yes*'s!) When you find yourself facing a choice between Source and socks (i.e., a Yes or a No), reach for the affirmative whenever you can.

Attitudes

Be Honest and True

A mom I know hasn't told her three preteen daughters that she was married and divorced (to someone who was not their father) before they were born. Another keeps mum about the problems cropping up in her marriage, even though the kids undoubtedly sense the tension. And a dad helicopters over everything his son eats to keep the boy from being teased as a "pork chop" the way he had been, but he keeps his "shameful" history to himself.

They excuse all of these behaviors and more by telling me that they are merely small, white lies. But no matter how tiny and colorless they may appear, a lack of truthfulness knots the relationship flow between parent and child. Lies are the foreboding cloud over a day at the shore, the unspoken darkness between lover and loved. Whether the tale is an outright fable or an omission of fact, it wordlessly communicates that you do not honor your child with your own truth.

Billy Joel once sang about how lonely "honesty" is in romantic relationships. I think it's even rarer between parent and child. As a society, we've institutionalized lying to kids, justifying it on their supposed inability to handle the facts. More likely, it's the parents who have trouble handling it, because most of the kids I know will understand and accept pretty much anything if it's told to them in a caring way.

It's not easy to confess to a sordid past; to worries and insecurities; to current problems with money, health, or your relationship. (Although kids are so astute I suspect most of them eventually uncover these secrets.) But when parents live authentically, they make their child a full partner in their lives, an act that transforms the relationship. What's more, being honest with a child encourages him to share his anxieties, anger, fear, and foibles. I'm aware that some parents say, "I don't want to know what my kids are up to, especially when they reach the experimental teenage years." But those things are actually the most crucial for you to know. What better way to get a meaningful dialogue going about drugs, for instance, than to confess that you once experimented with cocaine—or that your friend's life was tragically cut short by an addiction? A single mom sharing the dejection of a new boyfriend's rejection, even to a young child, almost guarantees that the child will open up to her mother years later when her own heart is broken.

I battled my desire to smooth over the truth when my kids were young. A coauthor I'd been working with on a book project, whom I found to be impossibly obstinate, scuttled the project after many months of work. I was angry about how much time had gone down the drain and a little bit ashamed that I couldn't make the partnership work, but my instinct was to suppress my distress in my children's presence. (You know the drill: "What's wrong, mommy?" "Oh, nothing!" she replies, artificially brightening.) But I understood the value of sharing my true feelings and of modeling the reality that defeat and disappointment are natural occurrences.

My friend Ted is among the many adults I know who explain away their fibs as useful for influencing a child's behavior. (Parents complain that kids are manipulative, but we adults are actually the masters!) Ted wanted his son to go to religious school each week because his own parents desired it, even though Ted didn't believe in that kind of God. Rather than be honest about his motive, Ted told his son it was required for kids to go. Sensing the deception and lacking a reason that resonated, the boy threw a fit every time. Contrast that with the experience of another friend in a similar situation, who confessed to his son that he didn't believe it was necessary, but shared how important it was to the boy's grandma that he get confirmed. The child was eager to oblige because he loved making his beloved Nana happy.

The first step in being brutally—or, rather, beautifully—honest with our child is to be frank with ourselves. I had to face down my fear of feeling like a failure before I could share the truth about that doomed book project. The once-overweight dad needs to embrace feeling lovable no matter how he looks before he can open up about his past to his child.

Importantly, honesty demands that you tune in to where your child is developmentally and share in a way and at a level that she can understand. Spiritual teacher Esther Hicks once used a wonderful analogy about meeting your children where they are by saying that you don't tell your 4 year old that one day her body will stretch really big and that she will move out of your house—even though those things are true. You may not want to tell your 6 year old that you were once arrested for shoplifting (perhaps more appropriate for 11 or 12), although you can mention at any age that everyone does things they later regret.

There may be nothing more powerful for a parent-child partnership than for mom or dad to let down the armor protecting their reputation and share who you truly are, disappointments and all. It's a process that takes time. But if today you open one tiny closed box of your hidden emotions or secret past, you'll be well on your way.

Attitudes

Nurture Their Wings

I was 9 years old when my older sister read me a story about a boy's canary: Someone had left the cage door open and the bird flew away; months later, while the heartbroken child mourned, the creature appeared at his window, contented by his time in freedom to return once again to his beloved friend.

I felt so moved by the love the pair felt for one another. But when I thought about the book in the following months, I couldn't help wondering: If the canary had not returned, would that have indicated he'd been unhappy with his prior life?

It took decades before the answer became clear to me: Moving on never negates the experience you are moving from. I left several wonderful romantic relationships in my twenties—which I wouldn't have traded for anything—that simply weren't right for where I was heading next. Over the years, I've also pulled back from a number of close friendships when what we wanted—or who we were becoming—changed.

As a parent, parting is built in to the agenda from the beginning.

Our kids were never intended to be with us forever (and, if you're honest with yourself, you wouldn't want them to be). But, especially at first, because they start off completely dependent, this is easy to forget. We may miss the signals that our child is ready—in small ways, initially—to forge an identity and a life that is separate from our own.

When a toddler clings relentlessly—as we try to cook dinner, blow dry our hair, or even take a shower—we may come to view togetherness as the natural state of affairs. But before you know it, that same toddler begs to sleep over a friend's, or your preschooler asks to accompany her older cousins to the mall, and our instinct may be to say no. Question that instinct (unless your child truly would be in danger).

I remember feeling stunned that my son's first-grade Montessori class was planning an overnight "camping" trip in the back of the school. Outside! Exposed to the elements! And with who knows whom driving by and finding all the defenseless little kids! (With teacher chaperones, of course—but no parents were allowed.) After the shock wore off, I realized this would be a great adventure for him and I happily let him go. He had a blast. Similarly, my neighbor pondered denying her fifth-grade daughter a school field trip to Washington, D.C., because she feared that tourist sites in the capital made for prime terrorism targets. (She also went, and also had a blast.) Keeping our child tight may seem like a wise approach, especially when fear rears its head, but it won't help her learn to unfold her wings and discover her power in the flapping.

Stepping back and empowering your child applies as well to the choices she makes for her life, even if her desires conflict with your dreams for her. Hard as this may be to accept, our kids are not in our family to satisfy us. Of course, it's impossible not to have ideals

63

for your child, but those plans must take a back seat to her own. This can be as important as what career she favors to as minor as whether she should accompany the family on a volunteer cleanup at a local park—a situation I faced when my son exclaimed that he wasn't coming along, even though I had committed all of us. I tried talking to him about how good it feels to give back to the community and about the value of protecting Mother Earth, but when he remained adamantly resistant I let him stay home with a sitter.

Sometimes, our children's fears mimic our own, but our role is to help everyone surpass them. In Rachel Naomi Remen's book *My Grandfather's Blessings*, she tells a powerful story of her first encounter with the Crohn's disease that would plague the rest of her life. While away at college studying to become a doctor, Remen suffered such serious internal bleeding it put her into a six-month coma. Once she began to heal, Remen returned to school, albeit with her mother because it was far from home and Remen was weak and underweight. After six months, mom announced she was returning home, leaving the frightened and still recovering Remen on her own. Years later, when the now-successful physician asked her mother how she could have walked away at such a treacherous time, her mother admitted it was hard. "I was terrified for you," Remen quotes her mother as saying. "But I was even more frightened for your dreams. If they died, this disease would have claimed you." Notice the mother said "your dreams." I have no idea if she also wanted her daughter to be a doctor, but mom understood that her goal was to facilitate her daughter's wishes.

Spiritual author Eckhart Tolle wisely advises, "If you have young children, give them help, guidance, and protection to the best of your ability, but even more important, give them space—space to be." Giving a child a very long leash not only leads to her happiness, it's more likely to foster success than actively pulling her in your chosen direction. When a psychologist studied top-flight musicians, artists, athletes, and scientists, he found that most were not pushed by their parents; instead, their passions were nurtured only after the child exhibited interest. I tell people I am certain I didn't push my kids in any career directions because one chose to be a computer engineer working on weapons systems, while the other is contemplating joining the Peace Corps after her college graduation.

I once saw a terrific comic strip where the drawing was split in two frames. In the first, a mother takes her son to kindergarten while the son grabs the mother's legs so he won't have to go. In the second, the mom is taking her now-grown son to college, and she's the one grabbing *his* legs.

That's all good fun, but if you've done your job well and let him go little by little, by the time you drop your child at his dorm you'll feel confident he is walking into an experience that he is more than equipped to handle.

Attitudes

Discipline From Your Heart

"Go to your room and think about the terrible thing you just did!" a mom-friend commanded her 6 year old after he purposefully threw his ball at her—hard. Muttering something inaudible but obviously unpleasant under his breath, the boy stormed into his room and slammed the door.

I sympathized with this frustrated mother. We've all been there: Helpless to stop our child's destructive behavior, yet casting about for how to respond. But my heart also went out to the boy. While he went to his room as his punishment demanded, I would bet my writing hand that he was not "thinking about the terrible thing he just did." If his mind was pondering anything in that moment, it was likely some angry (and unprintable) thoughts towards his mom.

As parents, we feel pressure to punish our child when he misbehaves. (These days, we typically call it a time-out, but it's punishment all the same.) We may fret that not delivering a strong response will sanction the behavior, fear being a "pushover" to a pint-size person, or worry that other people will think we're lax. Yet leaping into punishment rarely helps our child. Plus, meting it out is bad for us, since punishment resides in a low-vibration, disconnected place near judgment and vengeance.

I learned the value of seeking alternative solutions from two amazing preschool teachers when my son was four. He'd been going through a phase of flicking his fingers at friends and strangers, as if he were trying to zap them with an imaginary ray. More than one witness to this action suggested that my husband and I should put him in a time-out whenever he did this. But we resisted, sensing that he viewed the motion not as an aggression but as a shield, because he felt overwhelmed around crowds and this was his way of retaining emotional boundaries. Still, I felt conflicted, because I wanted him to stop.

During his first day at preschool, when he flicked at his teachers, they thanked him for sending fairy dust their way, pretending the invisible sprinkle sent them floating on air. Because they accepted (nay, cherished) the behavior rather than push against it, my son soon stopped, not only with them, but with everyone.

A more traditional punishment may have "worked" with my son. That is, it may have caused him to stop. But because he felt embraced by his teachers despite his action, they provided him with the sense of security the flicks had engendered. Another child similarly found that giving those same teachers his middle finger was met with them kissing it, also lovingly putting that behavior to bed.

I believe there's always a reason logical to the child about why she does unwanted things, even if we haven't uncovered it. Our goal as parents is to understand where our child is coming from when she lashes out or misbehaves. Perhaps she's feeling out of control, or unheard, or scared about something. Grabbing another kid's toy or screaming at the teacher is a way of taking back power, even if, from our wiser perspective, we know it's not the best way to do that.

The ideal approach for altering behaviors that are destructive or unkind is to guide our child to her heart. Harsh words and actions don't usher in gentleness; only a tender approach will awaken caring qualities in her. You yourself know that when you do something mean in your own life—at work, say, or with friends or relatives—you hope they will respond with love. Compassion instead of condemnation is no less important for your own beloved child.

Kids understand when they have done something cruel, and the natural consequence they feel after seeing another's reaction is often punishment enough—even if they're unlikely to admit that they feel bad. I remember as a 9 year old being so mad at my older sister (for some long-forgotten infraction) that I snuck over to her desk in our shared bedroom when she was out and hurled a foot-high statue of sugar cubes shaped like the Washington Monument to the floor, a tedious school project she had worked on for weeks. I felt exhilarated for a moment, but when she found her creation broken in two, tears poured down her cheeks. I immediately understood how heartlessly I had acted. No punishment could have produced as deep a feeling of remorse—although, of course I got one anyway from my parents, via a screaming lecture and revoked privileges.

Sure, kids still need boundaries and guidance. When we see them behaving in ways that let us know that their pipeline to Source is kinked and they are having trouble untangling, it is our job to assist. If their actions pose a danger to themselves or to others, we may need to more directly intervene. But to be lasting and loving, the re-steering of the wheel must ultimately come from inside the child.

The next time your child "misbehaves," even if the ball was thrown hard right at you, resist the urge to react with a scream, a swat, a punishment, or a privilege removal. (Time-outs, in the pure sense of the word, can be helpful if they're used merely to give all parties a chance to come back to their calm center before reacting.) If that's how your parents disciplined you, changing this pattern may take special effort. But as Jon and Myla Kabat-Zinn write in their book, *Everyday Blessings: The Inner Work of Mindful Parenting*, it can also be the most rewarding for the parent. "The irony is that we may come to experience completion, wholeness, and a healing of our own emotional wounds precisely by tending to the needs of our children in appropriate ways."

So it was with the woman who sent her son to his room that day. After much contemplation, the next time he did something similar she gently talked to him about how his action physically and emotionally wounded other people and, ultimately, himself. Rather than chipping at the bond between this mother and child (and between each of them and their higher selves), this process of offering loving guidance served to strengthen those ties.

🐚

Attitudes

Say Goodbye to Guilting

How many Jewish mothers does it take to change a light bulb? (Heavy sigh.) "Don't worry; I'll sit in the dark!"

Not all of us have Jewish mothers—and fortunately, some of ours aren't so melodramatic. Nonetheless, guilting children is a staple in many households. I'm convinced that had guilt not been experienced by Adam and Eve when they left the Garden of Eden, they would have discovered it soon after they had kids. Surely the world's first couple would have realized what every parent comes to know—that guilt is a fast and effective way of inducing compliance.

In my freshman year of college, my roommate's mother wanted her daughter to call her twice each day. This being the first time Claudia was away from her overbearing mom, she didn't share that desire. So her phone rang round the clock, with messages left along the lines of: "Don't worry, I'm all right even though I slipped on the floor and banged my head."

At the time, I laughed at this mother. But now I see her use of guilt for what it is: the brandishing of a weapon as harmful as a saber, maneuvered with almost as malevolent a result. By wielding guilt—that is, trying to induce their self-flagellation—we tell our child how we believe she should think, feel, and act, rather than letting her create these experiences for herself.

Parents, especially mothers, think they're the ones who feel too much guilt. About not spending enough time with their child. Or not having the resources to give the child everything she wants. But parents don't realize how much they actually try to induce this destructive emotion in their child.

For all parents, generating compliance through guilt—as with punishment—has its advantages. I'm sure Claudia spent her years prior to college behaving exactly as her mother wished her to. But if we're wanting our child to do something for us, we should get clear about our needs and ask directly.

I once read an article in a women's magazine by a mother who used to pour on the guilt when her young daughters didn't make their beds or clean their rooms. It was only after significant introspection at a spiritual retreat that the woman realized that she saw the girls' "disrespecting" her desire for cleanliness as a sign they didn't love her enough. She also realized that line of thinking came from *her* own mother. Soon she was able to stop inducing guilt and let her daughters maintain their rooms however they wanted.

My friend's mother actually called her to her deathbed to deliver a final life message: "I've lived with enough guilt for both of us," the old woman said. "Please don't feel bad about any of the choices you've made in your life, even if I or anyone else didn't approve of them."

Here are some parent guilt trips I've heard through the years:
• "Your father is going to be mad if you don't cut your hair short." This from a mom to her Samson-like adolescent in front of a barbershop. "I'll live with it," the boy responded. "But your dad might

not, with how weak his heart is!" the mom snapped back. I didn't hear the rest of the conversation, but the boy later emerged with a major shearing. The mother got her way, but I worry there was a cost to her son's budding sense of independence.

• "I told you that toy was cheap and would break after you bought it." When I overheard the smug father tell this to his daughter, she was in tears, eyeing the severed pieces of a plastic airplane strewn around the restaurant table. Where was his compassion at how sad his beloved girl was feeling? And will the girl feel confident in her choices in the future if he berates her on this one?

• "Your little sister may never want to swim again, after you terrorized her in the water!" I, too, had watched the splashing between the girls get a bit out of hand, but I doubt anyone was actually terrorized. A calmly administered, brief diversion from the water would likely have been sufficient, without making the older child question her love and kindness for her sibling.

Why do we feel the need to inject guilt into our disagreements? For starters, because it's easy. "How could you disobey what I'm wanting?" likely yields quicker results than, "Tell me why you wish to do it your way and we'll discuss it." And delivering a shame-inducing "I told you so," even to a helpless child, can trigger an oddly satisfactory sense of superiority. Plus, your parents may have resorted to guilt, so it makes sense that it may call to you.

But it's important not to scratch that itch. Psychologists say that most kids can't distinguish between their actions and their selves, so the guilt you bring forth in them becomes a dagger to their self-esteem. From a spiritual perspective, a guilt-inducing reaction comes from your disconnection from your higher self, which is pure love and would never seek to diminish someone. It also disconnects you from your beloved child; as she ages, she will catch on to your attempts at manipulation, as Claudia finally did, and start to see you in a different light.

Probably the most famous guilting mom is the one who peers out from the clouds in Woody Allen's 1989 movie, *Oedipus Wrecks*, ominously wagging her finger at her son's every turn. Thankfully, most real-life parents aren't that extreme. Still, the next time you feel the urge to lay guilt on your child, ask yourself if you want your child to see you as Woody's character viewed his mother. If not, take a moment to talk to your child, calmly and honestly, about what it is you want or need.

Attitudes

Trust Your Energetic Link

Well-meaning relatives and friends sometimes told my husband and me that we were wrong to let our kids sleep in our bed, to stop what we were doing to walk a child into a dark room in the house when they were afraid to enter solo, or to give each child the time he or she needed by staying for weeks with them at their preschool until they were ready to separate happily. We did those things because we believe our children's needs are as important as our own. But we also did it because we believe in treating them as we would want to be treated ourselves because on some level we *were* treating ourselves that way.

The teaching "do onto others as you would have them to onto you" is more than just about making nice, according to the spiritual philosophy I believe. It means we're all connected on an energetic level, so what you do to others in some way affects you, also. After she had a near-death experience from advanced cancer, Anita Moorjani, who subsequently wrote the book *Dying to Be Me*, says she understood during her time in the spirit world that each individual is like a finger on a hand, invisibly connected via the unseen palm to the other fingers (i.e., other people). On a plane we can't see, we humans are somehow linked to one another, so when one feels hurt it diminishes all of us.

How would your actions towards your child differ if you put yourself in her metaphysical shoes? "Let's try this exercise," I prodded some friends at the park some years back, while we were watching our children play in the sand. "Pick out a kid you don't know, watch him for 10 minutes, and begin to feel like you *are* that child."

"I've got that red-headed, freckle-faced cutie," one friend called out. Another picked an overweight, grade-school-aged boy. I selected an adorable Asian toddler. For the next 10 minutes, we watched "our" child go about his or her business.

The pudgy boy climbed up a jungle gym but didn't have the muscle tone to get back down. A few older boys walked by him and snickered. "Ouch!" my friend exclaimed in sympathy.

"Time to go, Krista," the Asian girl's mother soon called out. "One more minute, mommy, I have to finish making my castle," the child replied. "Sorry, honey, but I'm out of minutes," the mother said, swooping up the now-screaming girl and accidentally tipping over the sand castle. I winced, recalling an incident a week earlier when I had carted my own daughter out of a toy store just as brusquely. I immediately realized other ways I could have handled it that were more empathetic, such as telling her before we entered that she'd only have a couple of minutes or by promising that we'd come back to the store when we could spend more time.

Meanwhile, the freckle-faced boy was picking up rocks and handing them as gifts to other kids. The smiles on their faces had my friend elated. By amplifying her connection with the boy, she too felt the love showered on him by the other children.

Contrast this with the time I was in a pizza parlor when a woman started screaming at her preschool-aged son, "Don't you ever embarrass me like that again! When someone does something nice for you, say 'Thank you.'" The boy's eyes bulged in terror, apparently fearing that a smack across his backside might follow—and, indeed, it did. When I thought about this mother later, I wondered how differently she might have behaved if she'd felt that she was doing this to herself. After all, if she were the one who'd forgotten to say thank you to someone, wouldn't she want to be corrected with gentleness and love?

It doesn't matter if you believe as I do. Even if we're not *actually* linked to other people on a metaphysical level, why would we treat someone differently than how we would want to be approached? Shouldn't general compassion guide us to interact with other people, especially our child, with love?

In *The Little Book of Letting Go*, minister Hugh Prather observes that if we truly allow ourselves to feel united with our romantic partner, "we would never look down" on our partner's fears of flying, embarrassment, or aging. I believe that sentiment holds equally for our kids. When we allow ourselves to feel as one with our child, it must profoundly transform every one of our interactions.

🐚

Attitudes

Know They Are Perfect As They Are

The little boy was throwing blocks across the room (narrowly missing his playmates), screamed while others tried to hear the teacher read a story, and pitched a snack-time tantrum because he wanted to sit in an already-occupied chair. I watched a few other parents at my daughter's co-op preschool indicate their disapproval. But the teacher, a woman with a big heart and a deep soul, gently admonished us grown-ups not to judge. "They are a work in progress," she soothed. "It's all fine. Actually, it's perfect."

A work in progress. Aren't we all? And yet to see that work as part of a perfect picture is one of the most challenging—and critical—spiritual practices parents face. A colicky baby screaming into the night is perfect? A toddler ripping a hole through your expensive leather couch? A grade-schooler called to the principal's office for hitting her teacher? A teen who sneaks out to be with friends?

A wise sage once said that Source has a spot on a map just for you, and it's exactly where you are. The same, of course, is true for your child. That's why we shouldn't judge that child as bad or lacking because of his place on that map. Alas, judging is something most of us do most the time.

Breaking out of the mindset of judgment is challenging; it's such an integral part of American culture. The minute we leave a movie everyone asks, "What did you think?" When a new work appears in a museum, a crowd quickly gathers to assess its appeal. When we exit a restaurant, we typically proclaim whether we liked the meal and maybe even the people we dined with. People even ask parents in the first weeks after birth whether a newborn should be judged as "good" (meaning, in their view, whether he is quiet and sleeps well, as if an uncomfortable, unhappy baby somehow is not).

I once made it my spiritual practice to go an entire day without passing a single judgment. My plan was to observe and experience, without needing to categorize events or people into pleasant or unpleasant, satisfactory or disappointing. I made it through good-morning hugs with my young kids without deeming whether the moment was over too soon, and I saw myself in the mirror—hair spiking in all directions—with ease. But when I read an email from an editor indicating that he was still unclear about an upcoming project, I dubbed the man "stupid." Then I went further, berating myself for "failing" to complete my spiritual mission. I'd lasted a whopping 45 minutes.

It's no surprise, then, that when our children fall short of our grand plans and lofty expectations we judge them, too. Doing so, however, robs kids of the ability to know their magnificence, and robs us of the opportunity to have a mindful, loving encounter. There is a fabulous story by psychologist and mindfulness expert Jon Kabat-Zinn, coauthor of the book *Everyday Blessings*, about a man who heard Kabat-Zinn speak about the acceptance that had consumed him when his son came home from college one Thanksgiving, even though the young man arrived so late the meal had been eaten and the family was in bed. The man wrote to Kabat-Zinn that hearing the story allowed him to finally approach his own grown son nonjudgmentally, to fill up with unconditional love rather than the disappointment he had experienced for so many years. "It is as if up to now I needed another kind of son to love, and now I don't anymore," the man observed. How wonderful that the man could finally see his son as perfect—no alterations required. How wonderful it would have been had the dad seen him that way for all the years before.

"Presume every person's holiness," spiritual author Neale Donald Walsch writes in *Conversations With Good, Book 2*. Presume our children's holiness, he further decrees. "A tree is no less perfect because it is a seedling. A tiny infant is no less perfect than a grownup. It is perfection itself."

Seeing our child as holy takes only a flick in our perception. The facts stay the same, but an altered perception renders them anew. (As a little magnet on my refrigerator reminds me, "Attitude changes everything.")

Here's a great story of how much perception matters: Back when I was younger and single, I met a guy who told me he lived in an apartment with his mother. My mind labeled him an immature momma's boy and I started scheming how I could end our date prematurely. Moments later he elaborated—his mother actually lived with him. His father had died a few months earlier and he had opened his home to his grief-stricken mom. Suddenly, I saw him in a completely different light. In seconds, he transformed from pitiful to perfect.

Years ago I attended a spiritual workshop where an attendee exclaimed to a group of women seated nearby, "I could love you all if I knew your stories." An even more spiritually advanced practice, though, would be to love us all because she knows we do have stories, whether she hears them or not. Similar stories have led our child to the current, perfect place in her life. If I had said that the block-throwing boy at the preschool had just been diagnosed with leukemia—or that his father had—most of us would feel compassion instead of contempt. Why can't we experience that compassion no matter what?

Mary Sheedy Kurcinka, an educator and author of the book *Raising Your Spirited Child*, believes that parents most easily negatively judge their child when their temperaments are at odds. An extroverted father more easily belittles an introverted son. A tidy mother casts aspersions on her messier daughter. A low-key parent disapproves of her wildly energetic son. (Although I think sometimes we also have the most contempt for the traits in our child that we see, and hate, in ourselves.) Isn't it better to work towards embracing the differences between us and proclaim all styles superb?

Accepting a child as perfect doesn't mean ignoring your role as parent to guide him when he disconnects from his higher self, but this can be done softly. A perfectly wrapped gift might benefit when you tweak the bow. And a perfect child who doesn't understand that it's best not to leap off an unstable bookshelf may need a gentle explanation.

I'm reminded of a parable where a girl and her mother walk on the beach and find thousands of starfish washed ashore. The girl dashes about, trying to place some of them back into the water, but her mother declares that there are so many her actions won't matter. The girl stares at the precious starfish in her hand and declares,

"They will to this one." Today, no matter what your own starfish does, accept the perfection of his washing up on the beach—and know that it is equally perfect for you to gently and lovingly nudge him back into the water.

Actions

❧

"Love takes more than crystals
and rainbows.
It takes discipline and practice."
— Marianne Williamson

ও

Actions

Make the Birth Awe-Inspiring

Birth: The primal rite of passage for a baby—and an equally crucial one for mom and dad. It's only after our first child's birth, after all, that we become parents. The birth affords us a unique moment to deeply feel our child's connection to Source, and, by extension, our own. It's an opportunity to experience powerful rituals marking this sacred time. It's when we reassure our newborn for the first time that we are connected to him and are always available to help him navigate our complex world. It is one of the rare moments in life when we merge with all people, across time and geography, who have walked this path before.

Unless it is not.

If you give birth in America today, chances are that the main connection you feel is to a honking, beeping fetal-monitoring machine, your earliest communication with your newborn occurring through the cold glass wall of a nursery. Hospital births are often sterile factory events, the birthing couple mechanically propelled along a conveyor belt from the entry door through the monitors, drugs, episiotomy, and maybe a C-section, until a day or two later they're unceremoniously ushered out the door. And the rituals you're most likely to encounter—donning a hospital dressing gown, having heart monitors and blood pressure cuffs connected to your body—exist for the ease of the staff. Ensuring that you and your baby have a joyful, spiritual experience isn't their priority.

But you can make it yours. With a little planning and the right midwife or obstetrician attending your birth, you can boost the odds that the experience will be magical. (And don't let anyone tell you a highly medical birth is the only way to ensure a baby's health; except in rare circumstances, an enlightened birth and a healthy baby are not mutually exclusive.)

To better the chance that your birth will be the transformative occurrence you deserve, include spiritual aspects to your pregnancy as soon as you discover you're expecting, and as often as possible thereafter. When I found out I was carrying my second child, whom we tried to conceive for nearly a year (contrasted with one week for our first child), I hugged the pink test stick with massive appreciation, then lowered myself onto the bathroom floor and meditated for nearly an hour. My aim was to establish a connection with the soul of my child and to send gratitude and love in all directions. (I suspect my next-door neighbors wore big smiles the next day, even if they didn't know what hit them.)

As with most parents-to-be, though, I soon got distracted by the tasks of current motherhood (taking care of my 3-year-old son) and impending motherhood (gathering the infant clothes, furniture, and such that I would need). Fortunately, in my final trimester, the kicking baby woke me up to my spiritual focus, and I began a daily communion with the spiritual being I was carrying. I had some of my most powerful meditations ever, my sense of connection expanding beyond my baby to all beings in the world. Interestingly, in one meditation I felt myself telling my unborn child not to worry about anything, and had the distinct sensation she was telling me that it was *I* who shouldn't be concerned.

Renowned pediatrician William Sears recommends a nightly practice for expectant parents that I performed as well. Sears calls it the "laying on of hands." Place your hands on your protruding belly as you lie in bed just before falling asleep, using that connection to silently send love and acceptance to your child. Be open to what, if any, sensation comes back to you.

You can also celebrate your enhanced connection to Source by asking friends to hold an alternative ritual known as a "blessingway," either in addition to or instead of a baby shower. This blessingway (the name is apparently derived from a Navajo rite) begins when the mom is greeted by close friends holding candles and softly remarking on your strength and beauty. Each friend then takes a turn chanting the names of their ancestors, going as far back as possible (e.g, I am Meryl, daughter of Joyce and Joe, granddaughter of Kitty, Maxwell, Jean, and Abe, great-granddaughter of Esther, Lewis, Fanny, and Louis), to remind us of our bond to all souls, born and unborn, living and dead. Other parts of this uplifting ceremony include a warm herbal foot bath for mom, a crown of fresh flowers placed on her head, songs and poems about love and connection, and the serving of cake and tea. Social conversation and even practical baby gifts can be incorporated if the host desires. You can find details about this beautiful ceremony, which my girlfriends made for my second pregnancy, in the books *Mother Rising, Blessingways,* or others.

If all goes according to plan, the capstone spiritual experience will be the birth. I feel strongly that it is crucial to choose the right person to attend to your birth—not so much whether they are a doctor or midwife but whether they view birth as a natural and spiritual experience or only as a medical one. I was fortunate to have had magnificent midwives for both of my own special deliveries.

My first baby was born in a New York City hospital. My husband and I brought many spiritual props to the delivery room, including scented essential oils, small statues from our altar, and Sanskrit chanting music. We listened to my favorite, "Om Nemah Shivaya," a melodic phrase that means "I Salute the God Within You," over and over, which helped me to indeed salute the Source in everyone. When the baby's head emerged, I felt united into a single, magnificent whole: me, the baby, my husband, the midwife, the nurses, the women up and down the maternity floor, the residents of New York, really, all the people in the world. Time stood still—and it remained that way for hours.

(A funny epilogue to this story is that as I lay with my newborn that first night, I heard the entrancing "Om Nemah Shivaya" chants echoing softly from the hall. I couldn't believe that a Catholic hospital was playing spiritual Indian music! Only in the light of morning did I realize that the music had not in fact been piped over the intercom. I'd heard it so many times during my labor that it was playing in my head.)

My second child was born at home, which more easily allowed me to surround myself with incense, uplifting objects, music, and a whole library of spiritual books (which I believe are powerful even when they stay on the shelves). The soothing peach walls of my bedroom and the comfort of my own bed further facilitated union with Source. My daughter was born into a room filled with love.

The design of your birthing room and the props you bring into it can increase the odds of your birth being a truly spiritual experience. Famed French obstetrician Frederick Leboyer recognized in the 1970s that the cries of newborns after delivery might actually be calls of distress, owing to the harsh lights, cold room, and rough treatment they were subjected to. Leboyer didn't focus on a baby's—or parents'—spiritual essence, but he made progress in that direction. If you give birth in a hospital room that still sports the harsh fluorescents Leboyer largely succeeded in eradicating, bring a few colored silks to toss over the lights. Burn incense, sage, or essential oils, even for a few moments if the hospital frowns upon it, to make the air less antiseptic and more atmospheric. And by all means, play spiritual music (from any denomination that moves you). I know of a couple that even invited a swami into the birthing room to chant live during their birth!

Equally important is the welcome your infant receives after she is propelled from the warmth and safety of the womb. Leboyer realized that babies shouldn't be grabbed, flipped, spanked, and then whisked away from their parents. Today, most progressive hospitals and birthing centers immediately place the newborn on the mother's abdomen—but you might need to speak up if you want him to stay there a while. Some women prefer to give birth in a tub, so the baby goes from wet warmth to wet warmth, making the shift to the physical world less traumatic, and allowing the mom to remain in a more meditative state throughout.

Of course, a medical crisis, the excruciating pain of back labor, the true need for Cesarean surgery, or any number of other factors can conspire to drag your focus from the loftiness of Source during your labor or birth. If this happens to you, don't be angry with your situation; make even this occurrence spiritual by nonjudgmentally observing and accepting it.

The late Apollo 14 astronaut Edgar Mitchell, whom I had the pleasure of once interviewing for a magazine profile, claimed that hurtling through space in his tiny capsule was the most spiritual endeavor of his life. "I experienced what has been described as an ecstasy of unity," he wrote in his book, *The Way of the Explorer*. "I not only saw the connectedness, I felt it and experienced it sentiently. I was overwhelmed with the sensation of physically and mentally extending out into the cosmos. The restraints and boundaries of flesh and bone fell away." That's how I felt during both of my births. With desire, planning, effort, and, yes, a little luck, you can know a similar sensation.

~

Actions

Ease Your Newborn's Transition

"An infant sees only black, white, and red in the first few weeks," the saleswoman at the baby store told a very pregnant me, as I pondered various sheet designs for my first child's crib. "That's why these bold patterns are such big sellers." Those jarring, stark colors amped me up, but I assumed this woman knew more than a neophyte mom about how a baby's brain develops. I bought a mostly white-and-black clown pattern, accented with a few primary hues.

After my son arrived, I went to visit a friend and immediately got that I should have trusted my instincts. Liz had decorated her newborn's room in soft pastels with a Southwestern design. When I entered the room cradling my baby, following Liz with hers, both infants settled immediately. The peaceful glow of the light pinks, peaches, and greens relaxed all four of us—a striking contrast to the energizing sensation my clown pattern elicited. (Ultimately, my son wanted nothing to do with a crib, so he never did spend much time with that bedding.)

I'm sure I'm not the only parent to fall victim to the belief that babies can't really see, think, or feel. I've seen parents take an infant to a violent movie under the notion that the baby won't sense the negative energy emanating from the screen. Some adults even believe that infants won't remember anything. My friend's doctor was horrified when she refused to permit her 6-month-old son to have elective heart surgery. When she told him she wanted to wait until he could understand what was happening, the doctor claimed that he wouldn't remember a traumatic experience before age one. If that were true, why isn't it okay to neglect or even beat young babies?

I've come to realize the opposite: Babies are more attuned to their surroundings than we are. Her eyes may even be closed and her body sleeping, but on some level she is soaking up everything that's going on. My belief is shared by the early 20th-century Austrian educator Rudolf Steiner, developer of the Waldorf method of schooling, who taught that young children are huge "sense organs" receptive to all impressions from their environment.

Knowing you have this wide-open person in your home gives you the opportunity to become more sensitive yourself to the energy you are taking in. When I experienced my son's nursery decor through his perspective, it was obvious that I would never want my own sleeping space to sport such harsh hues. (Indeed, my current bedroom is a pale rose color.) My living room couch, however, had a few throw pillows whose jagged pattern I now saw was mildly irritating, so I tossed them away.

In her book *You Are Your Child's First Teacher*, Rahima Baldwin Dancy, an adherent of Steiner, offers suggestions for honoring your newborn's sensitivities: Choose clothing and blankets of natural fibers rather than synthetic ones. (Think about how fabulous it feels to wear a plush cotton or wool robe versus a polyester one.) Don't stock your home with plastic toys (which outgas plastic even when the baby isn't playing with them), and instead lean towards items made of wood, organic cotton, or felt. Since tactile sensations are important, I think parents should also be mindful to touch their baby throughout the day, rather than shifting him from plastic car seat to vinyl stroller to rubber play mat.

Breastfeeding and cosleeping (on a separate sleeping surface in the same room if you're worried you might crush her) also ease a baby's transition to our world, and they let you fall asleep kissing and holding a pure spirit. I remember how nursing transported my babies to another realm, their faces glowing with the most angelic expressions. I also recall how being around their blissful response elevated me, too. (Of course, there are reasons why some women can't nurse. If this happens to you, nonjudgmentally accept your reality and enjoy the bottle-feeding.)

Having a newborn in your home can also encourage you to think about spiritual practices you may want to incorporate into your life. During my yoga teacher training, I learned about the Hindu practice of *ahimsa*, or nonviolence towards everything. When my newborn came home, I became even less "violent" with how I opened a window, closed a door, placed a pan on the stove, or set a glass on the counter. I became so attuned to aggressive sounds that if a visitor banged a door, I startled like Meryl Streep's character in *The Bridges of Madison County*.

Perhaps the most important element in connecting with the Source your newborn has emerged from is to release your "to-do" list and simply sit with her. Infants are the best "be"-ers in the world. Rather than pull her out of this state, use her arrival as a reminder to yourself to enter that world more often.

ॐ
Actions

Tumble With Your Toddler

Your toddler leaps onto your lap every time you sit down. Takes every opportunity to finger-paint in her yogurt—or on your walls. Loudly squeals when the mood strikes her, including in a restaurant, religious service, or your elderly mother-in-law's apartment lobby. Sadly, in our culture we call this marvelous, uninhibited stage the "Terrible Twos" (which can actually run from ages one to four, or even later).

To a toddler—a happy-go-lucky being who hasn't yet learned the rule-oriented, fear-based, and behavior-obsessed aspects of our society—every moment is an opportunity for fun. Legs aren't for walking: They're for racing, hopping, climbing, jumping, and, mostly, skipping, the cadence that best expresses a child's joy. Food isn't to nourish the body: It's a plaything more colorful, textured, and varied than any toy—and no one shouts "no" when she puts it in her mouth to experience its sensations. Grass that adults trod over unnoticed is for picking, sniffing, lying on, and pricking on the skin. And pets: oodles of energy, softness, fun, and adventure—so like toddlers themselves.

There is an old saying that God couldn't be everywhere (of course, we know that "God," or Source, can and is), so he invented mothers. I believe that an equally appropriate quip might be that God couldn't be everywhere, so he invented toddlers. Seek to appreciate this great stage and to incorporate your child's exuberance into your own life.

Once, a mom in our playgroup watched my 2-year-old daughter toss dozens of colorful balls into the air, squealing as each one flew (and oblivious to the fact that someone would have to clean them up). The mom suggested making ourselves feel as free for the next hour. So there we were, otherwise prim adults, rolling around the floor, loudly clanging lids to pots, drawing on our hands and legs, and ripping bits of paper to make confetti. I hadn't laughed so much since, well, I was a toddler!

Before that day, I had actually looked forward to the time when my daughter would grow past this age. I wanted to walk through a grocery store without replacing all the boxes she'd pulled off the shelves. To go to bed without first having to stack all her blocks, shelve her books, and otherwise clean up her massive mess. To eat a restaurant meal without her jumping on our shared bench. Then I realized I was wishing away the greatest teaching I would ever encounter: That life is to be sung full throttle (if adorably off-key).

The next day I read an "improve your life" article in a women's magazine that advised parents to toss a blanket into the trunk of their car for impromptu play or picnics. I dug an old comforter out of the linen closet and stashed it along with sidewalk chalk, sand toys, and extra clothes for each family member. A few days later as my daughter and I were running an errand, we passed the beach. She went nuts when she saw the sand. Torn between my errand and our possible fun, I recalled the magazine article and the beach won.

We waded in the waves, buried our limbs in sand, created "houses" for the mermaids who might come out of the ocean and want to sleep (her idea), and dug deep holes in search of treasures hidden by ancient fairies (mine). We had a fabulous time—I would even describe it as a spiritual time, since I felt lighter and higher.

After that, I made sure to carve out time for us to play in mud, splash in water, pretend to be a seahorse, and dance to every kind of music imaginable. I engaged in these activities without worrying what else I should be doing. Being with a toddler also gave me permission to release my self-conscious fear of looking ridiculous, allowing me to tap into that place where unfettered joy resides. Psychologist Harville Hendrix observes in his book *Giving the Love That Heals* that adults often equate being silly with being vulnerable, and they avoid the former in an effort to stave off the latter. I believe that being silly is indeed being vulnerable, in the best and highest sense of the word. When we allow ourselves to be vulnerable, as sociologist Brené Brown observes, we open to our full selves.

For a toddler, the joy is in the *doing*, not in the *having done*. Reveling in the thrill of every action is its entire purpose, not a byproduct. I'm not sure exactly when—or why—humans decided that this fun-filled abandon is not the way we are supposed to live. Of course, a few people never learned that rule—and thank goodness for the Jimmy Fallons and Lady Gagas, for they serve as reminders to those without toddlers underfoot.

The next time you find yourself holding a pot and pan, don't immediately head for the stove. Clang them together, create a song to accompany your rhythm, and march or dance around your kitchen. Ignore any censors, outside or inside of you, who object. Then watch as your toddler (or older child) hoots to see you join his knowing that life is supposed to be a joy.

ॐ
Actions

Slash Your Family Must-Do List

When I was in grade school, my parents had a piano teacher come to my home. I wasn't a particularly talented player, although I could tap out a passable "Hey Jude" to impress my friends and "Für Elise" to please my parents. If my mother had asked me if piano was something I wanted to continue, I would have said no in a metronome beat. But she didn't, so I didn't. Hundreds of hours over many years were thus spent in a pursuit that satisfied no one (including, I'm sure, my piano teacher, who knew a half-hearted student when he heard one).

Today, gymnastics, soccer, and computer lessons seem to outpace piano in popularity, but the result is the same: Families fall victim to the curse of scheduled activities, at least some of which your child may not even enjoy.

Years ago my husband and I studied at an ashram, where we were fascinated to learn that a Hindu monk could spend an entire day cleaning a foot of his bedroom. One day for one foot! This may sound tedious, but the monks have figured out something frenzied parents would do well to understand: A spiritual life is a simple life.

When a family rushes to baseball on Mondays, trombone on Tuesdays, dance on Wednesdays, art class on Thursdays, and French lessons on Friday (not to mention ballgames, birthday parties, and religious classes on weekends), there's little time left to ponder, go inward, be spontaneous, or even stay with an activity that is making our heart sing. What's more, frenetic schedules hamper the ability to cherish the present moment even when doing something fulfilling, because we're aware that in 15 minutes we must stop to drive Sarah to softball or Becky to band.

Ironically, parents also overschedule our own calendars with events we believe are good for our child. A mother in the spiritual parenting discussion group I once participated in had three older kids and a young one. She said she helmed the PTA at her son's elementary school, joined the parent-advisory committee at the temple where her middle child would have his bar mitzvah, and took a part-time job to give her teen spending money. All notable endeavors ostensibly done for her children. Yet these activities robbed them and her littlest one of what they (and mom) need most, which is the intimate connection that comes from spending time doing nothing together. Our children (even our teenagers—and some would say especially our teenagers) require that bonding. Quality time cannot be scheduled on a rare free afternoon; it happens spontaneously when the energy of the universe somehow aligns to make a moment magical, and we are awake enough to notice.

To simplify your family's schedule, ask each person to make a list of their activities for the coming week. Include daily and weekly events such as school, work, soccer practice, and grocery shopping; one-shot items like buying a birthday present for your best friend; and anything else time is spent on, including your favorite weekly TV show or the half-hour you like to spend catching up on social media. Have everyone prioritize their list, then draw a red line two-thirds of the way down. Items falling below the line should not be accomplished that week. No matter what. Even if the person finds herself with a free hour on Thursday, right when that TV show airs, if that item is below the line they should skip it.

When someone first suggested this to parents in my discussion group, a room full of incredulous eyes stared at her. "Everything I plan is important, or I wouldn't be doing it in the first place," claimed a frazzled mom of four. "If I have the time to catch an extra exercise class, why shouldn't I?" challenged a dad. "How am I going to tell my kids there won't be groceries this week?" laughed another mom. Eventually, most parents gave it a try. When we met a few weeks later, we were all smitten with our simpler life. "Nobody noticed what I didn't do," the mom of four admitted. And while the dad had penciled three spinning classes high on his list—and attended them all—he agreed that squeezing in one more would not have been better than playing in the backyard with his daughter, which he did that evening instead.

When people find themselves with a free moment, too often they "kill" the time, rather than experience it fully. Yet as the writer Annie Dillard wrote, "How we spend our days is, of course, how we spend our lives." Resolve to pass any bonus minutes mindfully, by playing or talking with your child or simply observing her in action. If you are alone, resist the urge to pick up that magazine—or the mop. Meditate, walk outside, or sit and connect with the sky.

By scheduling fewer activities for the same amount of time,

you give grace a chance to enter your day. The knot in your stomach will relax as you realize you don't have to rush through what you're doing to get to the next thing, but can fully experience the moment—even when the moment involves waiting with your child at a gas station while they fix your car's blown engine hose (as one of mine did). People who spend their lives cramming in numerous activities lament how fast the years go by. But those who, like the monks, pass it with far fewer endeavors have the chance to savor each moment and, in a real sense, slow the time down.

ॐ
Actions

Make Silence Truly Golden

"Can't I please have some quiet in this house!" my dad would occasionally shout when his three shrieking daughters got the best of him. Since he was usually mild mannered, my sisters and I would take pity. We'd close our bedroom door or race to the backyard to continue our hot, gossipy conversation, allowing poor dad to have the quiet he desired.

When I reflect on those times, what strikes me is the opportunity my sisters and I could have had to use dad's admonitions to enjoy our own peaceful silence. It is an experience I did not want lost on my kids when they were younger, so we would at least occasionally use someone's plea for quiet as a reminder that silence is more than golden—it is a luminous path to fulfillment and joy.

Silence is the language of our soul. While we can connect to our higher self in spoken tongues—most easily via singing, chanting, prayer, and loving speech—one of the fastest routes to inner peace is outer stillness. That's because Source is always whispering to us, but we must quiet our minds to hear. Silence frees us from the need to talk about, and therefore categorize, what we are experiencing. "Being" quiet (note it's not called "doing" quiet) allows us to meet the hum of the universe that is too often drowned out with the louder—and harsher—babbling in our head.

In some religions, such as Quakerism and Buddhism, silence is an integral part of worship services. Spiritual seekers from Mahatma Gandhi to Mother Theresa regularly practiced silence, sometimes for weeks or months at a time. As the esteemed late yogi Paramahansa Yogananda once wrote, "Through the portals of silence the healing sun of wisdom and peace will shine upon you."

This is not to say that as a child I wanted to be seen and not heard. Some of my fondest memories involve yelling from my bedroom window to rouse my best friend who lived across the street; hearing my older sister shout my name from the basement to join her in our never-ending rounds of board games; and laughing wildly as my cousins, sisters, and I feebly attempted to square dance around our den.

Without loving guidance from a caring adult, though, children can live entirely in the world of noise. Silence may be seen as a torture to be endured during school or religious services, or when mom takes a business call at home. Teachers make things worse by using silence as punishment. Can't you recall your teacher saying something like, "Everyone will sit here without talking for as long as it takes for the person who stole the item to come forward"? Not understanding the peace that can be found in silence, I remember sitting painfully during those times, fidgeting in my chair, fixating on the clock, and feverishly trying to keep my thoughts from bursting over my tongue.

Many adults still view silence as an enemy to be conquered with sound. If a room is quiet when we enter, we may reflexively turn on music or the TV, pick up the phone, or talk to ourselves to fill the void. When we're with other people, more than a few moments without conversation can make us squirm. If we walk into a business that isn't bustling, we wonder, "Why is it so quiet here?" and consider going elsewhere.

Your family can transform silence into the most freeing of experiences. Silence helps everyone settle into a peaceful state. It also deepens interpersonal connection: Family members observing silence together may pay close attention to one another's needs, use touch as a form of communication, and have time to ruminate over issues rather than blurt out the initial, mindless response that strikes them. I remember when a swami acquaintance paused for several minutes before answering a question I had asked him. I was impressed with how he gave himself those moments to gather his insights before speaking.

If you're already mumbling about how you're never going to get your child to be quiet, know that resistance to silence is easily overcome once people experience its power. A yoga center I used to teach at regularly featured a day of silence, known in the Hindu tradition as *mauna*. Many people came into the center on that day as a skeptic but left admitting they had been moved.

Members of my spiritual parenting discussion group who agreed to give silence a go also praised it. As one mom said afterward, "Being silent with my kids reminded me of when they were babies and I would stare at them for hours without saying a word. I had forgotten how much love pours out of you when you're quiet."

Observing silence in the way I am suggesting is somewhat different from undertaking a sitting meditation (see "Try a Family Meditation"). In a formal meditation, you aim to still your mind by focusing on a single sound, image, or breath. Here, you quiet your tongue as you go through your regular routine. This heightens your other senses to the daily world, allowing you to experience the extraordinary in the ordinary.

Get together with your family and agree on the best day and time to try this—preferably one that is free from commitments and interruptions. A good way to start is during a meal. Mindfully eaten food tastes delicious, as your tongue ruminates over each exquisite bite. That's why ashrams and spiritual retreat centers often make meals a time of enforced silence.

You may want to start with an initial period of just 15 or 30 minutes to give everyone the opportunity to succeed. As your family comes to appreciate the practice, try building up to an hour or more, eventually reaching a half or even a full day. Longer sessions are tougher to hold together but are unbelievably enlightening. Everyone may come to love the practice so much that you'll want to schedule it regularly. One family I know observes a weekly Saturday morning silence from wakeup until noon.

Other types of non-spoken communication—writing, signaling, sign language—should be discouraged during silent sessions. Eliminating such "prattle" may be impossible at first. A family in our discussion group found that giving everyone a small note pad to jot down "important" thoughts they were dying to share helped during the transition. However, the notes were not passed around until the silent time was over.

It's best if everyone in your family buys in, but if someone balks, give her the freedom to opt out. She must agree, though, to respect others who are following the practice or to go to a friend's house for the specified time—and not to attempt to coax her little brother or her dad to utter a sound.

The first time I observed a period of silence, I was shocked—not by the quiet, but by the noise. My mind rushed to fill the stillness with jabbering, which rebounded around my brain as loudly as if the words had been spoken. In conferring with others since, I've found this to be common. We are so used to sound that our brain goes into overdrive to keep the tranquility away. After a while, the noises lessen (although they never stop) and the beauty of the silence blossoms.

Luxuriate in it. Listen to the sounds around you, from your child's sweet breathing to that always ticking clock you never noticed. Examine the auburn streaks in your daughter's black hair, the green in your son's finger-painting, your almond appliances—they're not really the color of an almond, are they? Pay attention to how your face feels to your fingertips. Your world will seem more vibrant than before, because when you shut down the avenue where so much energy escapes, it's rechanneled to the other senses.

Like so many spiritual practices, maintaining silence for even a limited time will feel odd at first, especially to your kids. I promise it gets easier. And the rewards—in terms of increased serenity and your family's more intimate ways of being with one other—are well worth the work.

🍥
Actions

Visit a Waterfall

A woman I chatted with at a grocery checkout line first turned me on to the idea of a weekly "green day," and she emphasized right away that she wasn't referring to the color of money. In fact, she elaborated, her family was aiming to not spend any cash one day each weekend, passing the time instead in the lush—and free—setting of nature.

I was immediately smitten, as visions of sunset hikes along the Florida beaches and canoe trips through the Everglades wetlands danced in my head. Then I quickly remembered why I hadn't done those things in what seemed like a thousand years: I had little kids! Yet so did she, and one of her babies was younger than mine.

Parents often let mental limitations constrict us more than our physical reality requires. Before we had children, my husband and I cherished walking in forests so dense we once mistook a massive rain cloud for the dark tree canopy overhead. (Did we ever get drenched!) We'd hiked to a breathtaking waterfall without a trail map, the charged ions of the misty air our sole guide. And if we didn't have time to drive far, we'd at least head to a nearby pond to, well, ponder our connection to water and the world.

Yet in the first years after our children were born, the most "natural" place we visited regularly was a local park. Not even the greener, earthier parts of the park, but the mulched-over playground and over-sprayed ball fields. By spending more time at the shopping mall than at the shore, I had denied myself and my family the chance to commune with the energy of the vibrating ecosystem of which we are a part. I had forgotten that trees, air, and water are as nourishing as tofu, asparagus, and watercress. So what if we couldn't hike for hours or paddle a canoe for miles? Once I opened my mind, I found a dozen places where we could go. "Family Green Days" officially went on our calendar.

One week later we got out of the car at a large nature preserve, which I had vaguely known existed but never thought to check out. Right away we saw a small baby alligator on the bank. My husband and I exchanged worried glances as our kids stood nearby; maybe we were out of our element after all. Fortunately, the gator quickly snatched up a crab and headed back into the water.

According to the trail map, an observation tower overlooking the 150,000-acre preserve of ponds and sawgrass—with what had to be dozens of varieties of birds circling overhead—was a mere mile walk over rocky ground. But after about 20 steps, I knew we wouldn't make it. "Carry me, mommy!" my toddler begged, startled by a beetle that was leeched onto her shoe despite her best efforts to kick it off. "Pick me up, too," my preschool-aged son demanded, glancing back to where the baby gator had been.

My husband and I futilely tried to get them to reconsider: Your legs will get strong from walking; we won't get to the tower with all those fun steps to climb if we have to carry you; staying close to the dirt is part of the charm. No luck. So I picked up our daughter and my husband lifted our son. We walked less than half a mile, until my arms nearly snapped. I put her down and took a seat on the ground. When my husband joined us, we realized that now, as always in life, we were already at our destination.

The four of us sat in that one spot for the rest of the day. The birds became our buddies, several showing us where they nested in the trees. Five-foot-high sawgrass danced in the breeze, choreographed to a Chopin minuet I could faintly hear. We got dirt under our fingernails scratching artwork into the earth. Many people passed us on their way to the overlook, but I'd let go of the expectation that we would get there, so I didn't care. Sure, climbing above this eerily unspoiled wonder would have been marvelous, but rather than an aerial view we saw tiny treasures on the ground.

A few weeks later we went to an area of Everglades National Park that has a tram ride. Seated comfortably in the open-air car, we meandered seven miles into the heart of the "swamp"—a word once as pejorative as calling an elderly woman a crone, but now embraced (ironically, as is crone) as a vibrant ecosystem that is, sadly, shrinking. We passed deer, rabbits, giant turtles, alligators, and numerous birds. A large anhinga bird stopped on a small log right beside us, stabbing his bill into the water and coming up with a flailing fish.

I could see awe on my kids' faces as they understood that the world equally belongs to these peaceful creatures, and that tuning to the environment opens our hearts. As we headed back to the now-crowded parking lot, I was hit with the same jarring sensation I used to feel years ago when my husband and I lived in New York City and would come back from our frequent trips to the Adirondack Mountains. After driving miles on roads lined with farms and fields, we would enter the concrete city. I would immediately feel my breath grow shallower as I switched from the rhythm of nature to that of man.

When the tram made its final stop and we gathered our things to disembark, my young daughter wouldn't move. "More," she said simply. Absolutely.

❧
Actions

Prepare a Feast

"Mom, how come you never let *me* cook dinner?" my then-school-aged son asked one evening as I was racing around the kitchen frantically pondering what to make. "Because you never asked," I replied, barely containing my enthusiasm. "You can cook right now!"

Of course, he wanted to make his beloved macaroni and cheese—and he wanted me to primarily cook it. Soon his younger sister rushed in, sensing more excitement in the kitchen than when I chop and slop solo. "I'll make the fruit," she announced, gathering up the green apples that were her favorite. "Let's make this a fabulous feast!" I suggested to a round of hearty hurrahs.

A fabulous feast. How many of us can describe many of our family meals that way? We've become a society where sit-down supper is almost a waste of our time, where food is often eaten on the way to sports games or lessons. Even meals in the home are gobbled with little thought or focus, on the living room couch or, worse, by the refrigerator, the food mainly an impediment to watching a TV show or making it to the ball field or library story hour on time.

Food is more than the fuel that charges our body so it can keep zooming. Food is our connection with nature and with our higher self—a reassuring sign that Source is providing the resources we need. (And if your mind jumped to, "Well, what about all the people starving in the world," remember that the world grows more food than all the people on the planet require, we just—so far—haven't had the will to ensure that it gets to everyone.) Eating lustily is a way to honor both the people who participated in bringing us the meal and the plants or animals who literally gave their all for it. What's more, eating with appreciation, especially in the morning, carries that mindset into the remaining activities in our day.

So I got out our fancy tablecloth and the kids decided to whip out the plastic party wine glasses and the floral cloth napkins. Recalling the waitress we had seen prettying up the napkins at a Thai restaurant the weekend before, my daughter asked if we could make ours into fans, too. I had been a waitress for a caterer back in high school, but I couldn't remember how to do it. After many flops, we wound up with a decidedly non-fan-but-nonetheless-unique decoration, which still looked nice.

The building excitement leading to our dinner reminded me of the day before Thanksgiving, when we prepare food for company. I realized that company was indeed coming—in the form of our higher selves. "Let's really pay attention as we cook," I suggested, "so we can make our dinner with love." My son began stirring the macaroni pot more deliberately while my daughter polished and carefully placed an apple on each plate. We fashioned a centerpiece out of drawings the kids had recently made. When my husband came home, we sat down to dinner.

We began by saying our version of grace. I decided to go beyond our usual, "Thank you Source and all the people who grew and prepared this delicious food." Stabbing a solitary noodle with my fork, I lifted it to my nose and sniffed. "I appreciate the delicious smell of this pasta and cheese," I said, smiling at my son. My husband and the kids chimed in, giving thanks for the way the ice crackled when the seltzer poured over it, for the soupy puddle the cheesy sauce left on their plate (the better to sop it up with bread), for the crunch the apples made when we bit.

We ate more mindfully than usual, and I must admit that even though I'm not typically a fan of mac and cheese, the meal tasted fantastic. While I had long heard the admonishment to eat slowly, and I knew that Buddhist monks make it a practice to chew their rice a hundred times (!) before swallowing, I hadn't done this in my regular meals. (Although I had eaten with better focus at retreats and ashrams.) During this supper, I noticed myself fully savoring every bite. Slow Food USA (yes, there actually is such a group, dedicated to eating as a cherished activity) would have been proud.

"How about a special dessert?" I asked when we finished eating, as much to prolong the experience as for a sweet treat. Since we didn't typically eat dessert, there was nothing in the pantry. Thankfully, my daughter dug into her leftover Halloween candy bag and pulled out some tiny packages of M&Ms. I opened a can of sliced pineapples and geometrically placed chunks on a dressy cake plate while she poured the little candies into the center. Sensing the divine in this dinner, my son and daughter lingered long after their plates were bare, rather than running off to get back to the video game and book each had, respectively, interrupted to come to the kitchen in the first place.

I wish I could say that event started weekly "feast nights" in our home. Alas, they became only an occasional occurrence. But, importantly, I began to see our regular meals from a more enlightened perspective. I put more intention into getting out the pots, cleaning the sweet potatoes, or draining the beans' soaking water. I set the table with gratitude that I had a family to feed and the food to do it. Connecting with my heart as I prepared each meal helped me feel uplifted—and I'd swear it made even the most basic recipe taste gourmet.

༄

Actions

Be Mindful of Media

Centuries ago, people sat outside staring at the stars, perhaps con-templating the meaning of the universe and their place within it. Today we're more likely to be inside, eating chips and watching "reality" TV.

That's generously assuming, of course, that we're not seeing some-one getting hacked to death with a machete. Studies continually report that violence in the media remains on the upswing, despite cries from critics to muzzle the mayhem. (I've always marveled at how graphic love scenes are verboten on TV, but murderous ones are acceptable, and how sex gets a movie an R or X rating but plenty of "family" movies are extremely bloody.) Since so little of what we find in our visual media can be deemed elevating, the best way for family members to connect to their highest and best self is to cut down on the viewing.

The American Academy of Pediatrics (which used to advocate for fewer than two hours of screen time daily for kids aged 2 and over until it finally gave up on imposing limits no parent could follow) blames media gore for aggressive behavior, desensitization to violence, nightmares, and kids' fears of being harmed. One landmark study, published in the prestigious *Archives of Pediatrics and Adolescent Medicine*, found that children who reduce their intake of television and video games become less aggressive in their class and playground (not as much "Give me that!" or "You want to fight?") than kids who keep their viewing habits steady.

On average, American kids spend more than four hours a day in front of the TV, according to the Nielsen Co., and something like seven hours total with their various screens. While screens of all sizes have become an integral part of all our lives, I'm convinced that watching this steady diet of violence on TV shows, streamed movies, and certain video games has to harden our heart from its natural state of love, detaching from emotions like compassion (or else how could you watch?) that don't flip back on so fast when you click off the remote. After seeing someone get beheaded in a drama or even a cartoon, how can you maintain your vision of humanity's highest potential? Glorious people who do glorious things are rarely characterized, which may partly explain how the "boob tube" got that name.

Introducing more unstructured, real-world activities better allows your family to reclaim a higher view of humanity and to more often take in the beauty of the world. If you eliminate even one media-hour each evening, that's a full seven hours a week. You can use that time for family reading, baking, impromptu playing, meditating, walking, or simply being in the presence of your loving kin. It's a gift of time that's yours for the taking.

Similarly, when you go out for dinner, instead of always loading a movie onto the iPad or handing over your cell phone to keep your child entertained at the table, mix it up with other, old-fashioned playthings. Table games like launching sugar packets over fingers shaped like goal posts is a classic. And there's always conversation.

Some people think families should watch television shows or streamed movies together as a way to spend time in shared pursuits. That's fine for the occasional entertainment, especially with high-quality, non-violent shows. But what a sad commentary if simultaneously staring at a screen flickering with images of baseless humanity is the best we can do to foster togetherness and love. Trust that when you hit the off button, more uplifting activities will fill the void.

∽
Actions

Pretzel Up With Family Yoga

I remember my first yoga class as vividly as if it were weeks ago, instead of more than two decades. Actually, what I recall is the going to and coming from that first class. Details of the session itself are a blur. What I easily conjure is the tension in my shoulders and stomach as I raced to the gym on my lunch break during that particularly harried day, visions of papers piled on my office desk swirling in my mind. Cars honked and pedestrians nudged me as I navigated the frenzied New York street crossings. Smog filled the air and vendors loudly hawked merchandise from the street corners, the cacophony further fraying my nerves.

When I entered the room in my gym where the yoga class was held, I felt desperate for a little soothing. After a variety of stretching and strengthening movements and calming breathing, the class concluded with a deep relaxation. I remember envisioning myself lying on a puffy cloud in a placid sky. When the teacher signaled the end of the session by ringing a soft bell, I felt connected to my higher self in a way I'd never experienced before. As I headed back to my office, the cars were still honking, people still jostling, smog still making it hard to breathe, vendors yelling just as loudly. But I felt removed, encased in a bubble of tranquility that nothing could disturb. I went back to my stack of papers and finished the day with a sense of calm.

The class had been even more than I'd hoped for—and my expectations had been high. I had decided to try the yoga class because a few days earlier at the gym I had been pedaling away on my exercise bicycle when the yoga teacher walked by—or, I should say, floated by. She moved like a gazelle; serenity personified. Although she was solidly middle aged, she looked young and limber. What's more, her inner peace radiated out like the glow from a soft light bulb. I wanted what she was offering.

Over the next few years my husband (whom I actually met at a lecture given by the late yoga master Swami Satchidananda) and I took many classes, ultimately becoming certified yoga instructors ourselves. Then we had babies, and our beloved yoga fell victim to time. Once the kids got a little older, though, we were able to get it together enough to incorporate yoga at least occasionally into our family's routine.

Doing yoga with young kids is obviously different than being in a room full of focused adults. But experiencing yoga with your family offers its own rewards, with the practice enhanced as you breathe and move together.

Children can actually begin to do yoga at any age (after their first months of life when they have little control over their bodies). In fact, a trend of "baby yoga" classes popped up some years back, although I'm not sure it's still prevalent. It's not that babies need yoga—they are born naturally flexible—although gentle yoga movements can help flow energy (and gas!) through their little bodies. It's that baby yoga, like that for older kids, is a terrific way to strengthen the bond between parent and child.

Once kids reach preschool or grade-school age, they are ready to take full advantage. Most kids naturally take to the way many poses imitate animals, from lions and snakes to monkeys and crows. Wonderful resources for yoga moves to do as a family include Marsha Wenig's *YogaKids* DVD and Mariam Gates and Sarah Jane Hinder's book, *Good Morning Yoga: A Pose-By-Pose Wake Up Story*.

When my daughter was young, she and I took our mini sessions one step further. Modeling our joint practice after "partner yoga," typically done with similarly sized adults, we adapted a few physically interconnected poses that we could do together. Maybe you'd like to give our favorites a try:

• *Helpful camel:* "Stand" on your knees, facing one another, and take hold of the other person's hands. As you both inhale, arch your backs (bending in opposite directions), your faces looking up to the ceiling in your quest to make camel humps. Breathing deeply, hold for as long as comfortable, then gently pull each other up by the hands. (Giggles at this stage are fine, and make the pose fun!) Repeat several times.

• *Loving turtle:* Sit facing one another, legs straddled wide, your feet nearly touching your child's. Both of you bend the knees slightly and bring the forearms from the front under the knees. Lower your head towards the ground. As you simultaneously inhale, each lift your head, neck, and upper back toward one another. Don't be shy about making eye contact or even blowing kisses. After a few moments, return to your "shells." Repeat several times.

• *Adoring cat:* Come on all fours, facing one another, knees under the hips and hands under the shoulders. Interlock your "paws" with those of your child's and flatten them on the floor. As you exhale, simultaneously round your backs and tuck your chins towards the chests. Hold briefly. Next, simultaneously flatten your backs and bring your heads level, gazing at one another and silently sending your love. Now, as you inhale, each continue raising their head upward and curving the back like a stretching cat. Continue alternating rounding, flattening/gazing, and curving several times.

• *Resting snake:* You can do this with as many children as are around. The first person (usually the adult) lies on his back, legs extended and arms resting gently by their side. The next person puts her head on the first person's abdomen, also assuming a relaxed position. Continue until all children have their head on another person's belly. The last child can put a favorite stuffed animal or doll on his abdomen. Everyone closes their eyes, breathing deeply and raising the tummy as they inhale, lowering as they exhale, all the while sending love through their belly to the person resting on it, and to all the others in the snake chain. Continue for several minutes.

You may find that your child loses interest in the yoga after a few minutes, especially the first few times. Part of the practice of yoga is acceptance of what is—whether that's your body's inability to stretch as far over your legs as you'd like or your child's desire to jump on your back if you continue your practice after he's finished. Sending out loving energy rather than frustration during these situations is even more true to yoga than doing a headstand or other challenging pose. I learned early on that most people think yoga is about flexibility, but it's foremost about flexibility of mind, not body. Embrace whatever comes out of your family sessions.

I like to end a yoga practice with deep breathing, which further quiets the mind and connects us with our higher selves. Sit cross-legged, back-to-back with your child. To do a simple breathing exercise called three-part breathing, each of you takes a long, slow inhalation through the nose, filling up the abdomen and puffing it out like a balloon. Continue taking in air, expanding the mid-chest region. Take still more air until the upper chest expands. Exhale slowly in reverse order. Repeat several times.

Although I treasure my adult yoga classes, the time I spent sharing this practice with my son and daughter (she hates the practice now—something else I have come to accept) were my favorite yoga moments. After even a short session with my kids, I felt that same bubble of tranquility that I experienced after my first yoga class in the gym—but now I had my precious children inside it with me.

༈

Actions

Give Meaning to Rituals

When our first child was born, my husband and I held a standard Jewish ceremony called a *bris*, which is a combination blessing, naming, and circumcision. The ceremony was pleasant enough (except for the circumcision!), and it was nice presenting our newborn to our relatives and friends, but deep down I found it lacking. The leader of the service, known as a *mohel*, recited his memorized script, something about the spiritual obligations we new parents were now facing. His words didn't seem up to the magnificence of the life that had just graced our family. When the ceremony ended, I wanted to shout the message the *mohel* neglected to impart: "*This precious angel has entrusted himself to our care, which will forever change my husband's and my views on love, humanity, and Source!*"

The birth of a baby may be second only to death in the number of rituals the various religions have created. But these officially sanctioned rites often miss the mark, especially since the core participants (parents) are typically reduced to spectators handing our precious bundle over to the elders of the tribe.

I couldn't help but contrast this ceremony with the deep-hearted welcoming event that our yoga center hosted for our son a few months after his *bris* (momentarily placing the baby up on their altar) that was so touching I actually cried. Or with a ritual that a friend crafted when his own son was born several years after mine. Since he and his wife had decided against a circumcision and therefore had no need for a *mohel,* they were free to create a rite that touched them. The parents spoke of their joy that a pregnancy finally happened after years of infertility, and they emphasized the baby's connection to their community by giving small speaking parts to many in attendance. In addition to traditional ritual ingredients like bread and wine, they added others, including candles and candy. I left their home that day feeling deeply connected to them, to their child, and to Source.

Rituals serve a crucial role, connecting our life's events—major turning points like the birth of a child or mundane acts such as eating supper—to the energy of the universe. Properly developed rituals encourage us to carve out a sacred space in our otherwise secular lives. The problem with the rituals most of us learned in religious school is that we do them with a rote unconsciousness that reduces their benefits.

Some people say that reading your child a daily good-morning story or giving her a nightly bath is a ritual, and I agree that anything repeated frequently is sort of one. But the rituals I'm talking about involve bringing an intention for spirituality to the experience. It was only after I committed myself to my made-up ritual of bathing my new baby with the reverence of Jesus' disciples washing his feet, for example, that I felt the bath-time transform. Sure, every so often I had to remind my "master" to stop kicking water out of the tub, but then I'd resume my mindset of awe. I completed my devotional action by gently wrapping him in his towel—and in my love.

For a ritual to be lasting, you have to enjoy it. Here for inspiration's sake are a few I adore. They mark varying milestones and can be done by a busy family. Include them in your life only if they touch you; if not, read books on rituals, brainstorm with friends, or just let your creative juices flow until you develop some that do.

• *Discuss blessings during dinner.* After the grace over the meal and before the mundane conversation, each person shares a special accomplishment or something he feels especially blessed about. This can be as simple as having seen a beautiful sunset or having surpassed a personal pace for running a mile. One family I know breaks out a journal once the dinner plates have been cleared to record any blessings a person wants inscribed. After a time, when this "blessing book" is filled it is placed on the bookshelf for reviewing when someone is feeling down.

• *Perform a family visualization before bed.* I'm crazy about the book *Starbright: Meditations for Children* by Maureen Garth. It features bite-size visualizations that are great for both kids and adults. For years I aimed to read one aloud each evening before my kids went to bed (my husband would close his eyes and join in). During these visualizations, you pin your concerns on a "worry tree" before heading into a magical garden accompanied by your guardian angel. There, you meet butterflies, fairies, busy working ants, or any number of fabulous creatures that encourage and inspire you to join their world. When my kids fell asleep, I was sure that visions of cherubs—not images of fighting superheroes—were dancing in their (and my) heads.

• *Welcome your ancestors to the holiday table.* A woman I know sets her family's holiday table with many objects from her family's history, from Granny Ethel's monogrammed bread tray to Aunt Evelyn's pickle dish. A toast welcomes these loved ones to the celebration, which is a marvelous way to reflect on the chain of connection that unites all humans, living and dead. When my own grandmother, and, later, my father-in-law, passed on, I made sure to get their holiday candlesticks and other ritualistic objects, which I always use as special-occasion centerpieces.

• *Hold "accomplishment" events.* Whether it's weaning your child from the breast or her mastering a level of acrobatics, endings are powerful. So, too, are beginnings, which tell us we're on our way to creating our next self, be it our first long sitting meditation or the first time your toddler donates old toys to underprivileged children. Design an event around these turning points to create a tangible demarcation that you're releasing the old and moving towards your new self-creation. In her book *The Joy of Family Rituals*, Barbara Biziou suggests forming a circle around the person reaching the milestone. After she shares her feelings about the accomplishment, everyone showers her with rice or confetti. Biziou advises that you can also immortalize the event by having the celebrant paint a fabric square with his name, date, event, and any words or drawings he's inspired to create. Glue each fabric to one large, wood-backed canvas to remind each person where he has been and where he's choosing to take himself.

• *Schedule regular rebalancings.* Adapted from the Hawaiian practice of "making right," this ritual emphasizes that when one of us is out of harmonious balance, we all are. Light a candle, make a talking stick (you can do this with your child: gather a twig and decorate it with feathers, beads, stone, and ribbon), and say a brief prayer. Then encourage each family member to share, in turn, whatever concerns her. Others then offer words of compassion, empathy, or concrete suggestions (if requested)—but no judgment or condemnation. Before passing the stick, members energetically send the person acceptance, forgiveness, and love.

• *Honor the passage to adulthood.* Although my children balked at the idea, so we didn't do it, I love the notion of a nonreligious coming-of-age ceremony around puberty. In Bernard Weiner's book, *Boy Into Man,* he describes the weekend event he and his friends held in the woods for their new teens, which included physical challenges, a theatrical production, and heart-to-heart conversations to welcome these young men into the adult world.

You may feel strange as you introduce a new ritual, but I suspect that when a priest-in-training first puts a wafer into someone's mouth or a new rabbi tells a groom to step on a glass, it feels odd to them too. It's okay to acknowledge your feelings, and in fact if you don't respect them you likely won't be able to go through with the event. Just remember that ceremonial actions are meant to be out of the ordinary; otherwise, they wouldn't make the imprint we intend. If you fear that your family won't treat these events respectfully, just keep your aim pure and your attitude purposeful. In the face of your commitment, even the most resistant child will likely come around.

๛
Actions

Put a Spiritual Mark on Birthdays

When a baby is born, a spirit comes into our world. How do we mark that awe-inspiring day in future years? By serving pizza and cake while a giant mouse leaps around a tumultuous room. The day becomes one of parties and presents, while the anniversary marking the moment our child's soul blessed our life is lost in the shuffle.

I'm not suggesting that parents abandon the usual festivities. My children would have been furious when they were younger if I'd told them we'd be skipping the party. Anyway, celebrations are fun, including those with a giant mouse. But, as in the chapter above, spiritually marking a major occasion—and none is more key than the anniversary of a birth—transforms the event. Why not add a small, sacred moment to the big hurrah?

Here I offer a few ideas, but as always, use your own intuitive wisdom to plan what works for your family. Such a ritual can be done early in the morning before the birthday rushing around begins, or, alternatively, at the time commemorating the child's actual entrance into our world. If you think these suggestions are weird, ask yourself if they're any sillier than blowing into a noisemaker or donning a pointy party hat.

• *Tell the Spiritual Birth Story.* Spiritual author Neale Donald Walsch says that each moment in life offers the opportunity to recreate ourselves into "Who We Want to Be," even if that person differs vastly from who we currently are. Our child's birthday provides the perfect time to reflect on that truism. Begin to get yourself and your child in the mood by playing gentle chanting music, holding rose pedals or other soft item between your fingers, and filling the air with scented herbs or incense. (Many herbs have symbolic meanings, so you can choose them consciously to reflect your intention; for example, sage fosters wisdom, basil enhances courage, and rosemary is the herb of remembrance.) After a brief moment of silence to connect with your center, start to tell the story of your child's birth from the perspective of your higher self (e.g, the thrill of helping another soul enter this world, the union of your highest essence with that of your newborn, the joining with Source experienced by everyone in the room). Then tell the birth story again, this time from the vantage of your child's higher self, or if he is old enough, he can tell this story himself (e.g., how pleased he was to come into this world and this family, how loving it felt to be held in his parents' arms). Because a spirit doesn't care whether there were physical difficulties during the birth, this should solely be an uplifting tale of love and connection. Finally, the other parent, older siblings, and anyone else who was present for the birth can add their own spirit's perspective. As you conclude, remind your child that we can always be "rebirthed"—that is we can remember, and live from, our Source connection at anytime.

• *Offer Spiritual Birthday Wishes.* My friend's family spends a few minutes during her child's birthday helping her set spiritual goals for the coming year—much as people make personal resolutions on New Year's Eve. This ceremony can involve parents, siblings, and any other special people in the child's life. Everyone sits in a circle with eyes closed, hearts open. A candle representing the light of the soul is lit and is held by whoever is speaking. Each person, in turn, tells the birthday child her thoughts on how the child's presence in the family has aided her spiritual connection, such as how the child's desire to help wounded animals reminds that person how important all life is, or how the child's ability to ignore being teased at school teaches us not to take anything personally. Everyone then offers a wish for the child, both for the next year and for many years to come—not so much wishes for material riches or accomplishments (although you can say that, too), but the hope that she remembers that all events can be seen as blessings and all people as part of Source. Finally, the birthday child states her own spiritual goals for the coming year, such as to be more loving towards someone he is having conflict with or to smile more at people he passes. The session ends with a loving group hug.

• *Enlist Some Twisted Candles.* Here, each candle on the birthday cake is joined to an adjoining candle by entwining the wicks of the pair. (Unlike with a traditional cake, there is no limit to the number of candles you can use.) The parent (or child, if he can handle matches) lights each pair of candles, acknowledging the way we are all connected to one another. Since a child's deepest union is to the mother who birthed him, as the first one is lit he acknowledges his bond with his mom. The child then acknowledges a similar link to his father, and to others in his life in the past year (teachers, friends, relatives, pets, neighbors, and even strangers who made an impression). Since the lighting of each candle severs the wicks' connection, this reminds to the birthday child (and everyone present) that even though people look separate we are all joined on a higher plane that isn't obvious in our physical world.

❧

Actions

Serve Tea

Early in my freshman year of college, I realized I was never going to be a coffee drinker. I had downed two cups before my job at the campus bookstore and soon my fingers were trembling so incessantly I couldn't press the numbers on the register. Because hot beverages are such an integral part of American culture, I didn't want to miss out entirely. I decided to take up tea.

At the time, and for many years after, I viewed tea simply as a soothing drink, a pleasant pick-me-up at the start or end of a tiring day. I made my cup with about as much forethought and ceremony as I brought to brushing my teeth: a few quick dunks into an old, stained mug and I was off and running.

I knew the Japanese make tea into an art form, but that seemed as foreign to me as bowing and chanting before a cup of cola. Then one day a friend dragged me to a tea-ceremony demonstration at a local Asian museum. I was stunned by the sacredness of a moment that until then I had viewed as the pedestrian mixing of water and weeds.

The Japanese ritual, more than 400 years old, aims to create simplicity through complexity; in other words, to know the rules surrounding the making and pouring so precisely that guests are freed to empty their minds. It was tea as meditation!

I didn't give it much additional thought until my then-young daughter asked me to "play tea" with her one day, using the plastic set she'd been given by her grandma. Memories of that Japanese ceremony came flooding back to me. With a little tinkering, I wondered, couldn't we elevate our own teatime into a meaningful ritual?

During our next trip to the library, I stole away from the children's section to do some quick research. Next to the Japanese books were some on the English tradition of afternoon tea, a rite begun in Queen Victoria's day. I wondered why the American pioneers didn't carry over this elegant and charming custom. Did they view it as part of the stuffiness from which they were eager to escape? Maybe, like us, they were too harried getting through the day to bother. Or, perhaps, once the Revolutionaries dumped the goods into the Boston Harbor and watched the crystalline water turn murky, they could never see the beverage as beatific again. Too bad.

While I think the tea-and-scones approach is delightful, I was viscerally pulled to the solemn, spiritual viewpoint of the Japanese. There it was, page after page in those library books, ritualizing each aspect: guests approaching the tea house on their knees as an expression of humility; everyone sitting on a small mat before a table decorated with a single flower; napkins folded crisply on the diagonal with the crease pointing exactly upward; and the tea master's precise steps, from wiping the kettle with a cloth to carefully scooping the ground leaves into a ceramic bowl, whisking the tea and water into a frothy drink, and placing it, bowing, before the honored guests. The recipients then bow back, cradle the bowl with both hands, and take long, slow sips while leaning away.

Since I believe that any act performed with inward focus and a sense of service is a spiritual one, I was impressed that the Japanese had figured out how to do this with tea. The official ceremony is quite complex, and perfecting it takes years. As one tea master commented in one of the books, "It takes a long time to learn the value of nothing." Still, I reasoned, even if we got a little something out of our meager attempt, it would be worth it.

The next afternoon the kids and I drove to a nearby Asian market I'd passed many times but had never entered. We picked up the essentials: bowls, whisks, and, of course, tea. Back home, I considered using the beautiful tea set given to me by my beloved late Aunt Jeanne before she passed on, but its floral print conveyed "party" more than "purity." My aim was to use the Japanese ritual as a springboard to help us connect to Source, to lift a secular snack into a meditative moment.

The kids and I set about preparing for our *chanoyu*, the Japanese word for their ceremony, although tea masters would blanch at our improvised interpretation. We played spiritual music in the background, lit a scented candle, and set our table with a delicate bud we'd snipped from our backyard. Of course, I was the "master" handling the hot water; the kids were thrilled to be guests, shuffling to our coffee table before sitting on some pillows. Instead of traditional confections made of bean paste, we served homemade sugar cookies on my daughter's plastic toy plates. When the water boiled, the kids sat mesmerized while I measured, whisked, poured, and served.

I can't say exactly what they got out of the experience the few times we did this, except that they were always peaceful for the remainder of the afternoon. I know that I found it enlightening. The simplicity, silence, sitting with my children in calmness, and the chance to focus on the moment and the blessings in my life were divine. And so was the delicious tea.

&

Actions

Hang Uplifting Art

Some time ago I looked at the pictures hanging on the walls of my home and realized I had purchased exactly one of them: a placid depiction of the port city of Jaffa by an Israeli artist. The print's gold and pastel buildings and the patiently waiting rowboats neatly tied to the nearby dock spoke to me of possibilities—of exploring new places, connecting to people across the world, and recalling the leisurely time before electronics sped up our lives. Six enlarged nature photographs I had taken during a pre-baby trip to Hawaii lined one hall. Everything else was on the walls simply because it filled up empty spaces.

Unless you're an art aficionado, perhaps you've gathered your decor the same way I did: a few castoff paintings from my parents' old house, gifts from well-intentioned friends, and the majority of items amassed as people we knew moved or redecorated. It is not that the art I ended up with wasn't lovely; it simply didn't speak to my soul.

I've since become a believer that the walls of our home are the altars of our personal sanctuary. Even if we're so familiar with what's on the surfaces that we no longer consciously see it, the energy they emit is absorbed into your family's every pore. We may not take in that painting in our kitchen as ravenously as we do the chocolate cake, but by taking it in slowly over time it can give us even more nourishment—or clog up our arteries to a greater degree.

I've always loved walking into New Age stores, churches, and temples because the artwork there feels so uplifting. Even if the images are not from my own faith, the simplicity of the work and the inspiration with which they were obviously crafted stirs me. Why shouldn't the pictures in my home fill my family with that same emotion?

So I took down a painting in my home office of a British streetscape that my aunt won years ago as a door prize. This left a gaping space on the wall, but the busyness of the scene had always clashed with the peaceful energy I try to cultivate around me when I write. I didn't have a budget for new artwork, so I trusted Source to fill up the wall. I gave away the picture and waited. Two weeks later my mother called (I hadn't said a word to her about my art plans) to ask if I wanted a framed poster from Florida's famed Coconut Grove Arts Festival. In her work in real estate she'd been charged with removing items from an abandoned foreclosed apartment. I immediately sensed that the poster, a collage of nature photographs from a single rose to a medley of rocks, would inspire creativity in a way the other picture never did.

When catalogs came in the mail from spiritual organizations, I suddenly noticed the art they were selling. I'd scour the pages for prints that moved me, and, over time, ordered a few. Now when I walk into my kitchen the first thing I see is a figure performing the 12-step yoga sun salutation beneath a rising red fireball. Over my bedroom altar (see "Create a Family Altar"), I enjoy a redheaded goddess delighting in a colorful butterfly garden. My bathroom features the restful scene of an outdoor Victorian garden seemingly awaiting the ladies who will luxuriate in it. (As I dress each morning, I fancy myself to be one of them!) Most recently, I bought an oversized canvas painting of a yellow flower for our breakfast nook, which gets us off to a sunny start no matter the outdoor weather.

Look around your home with a critical eye and see what messages your family members are absorbing. Does your artwork make you feel peaceful? Inspire you to connect with Source? Urge you and your family to be in the now? Making even one simple change—such as replacing an aggressively red abstract with an image of a gentle sea—can profoundly shift your ability to live and to parent in grace and love.

"Since I gave away a fussy piece of art, I feel calmer when I walk into my bedroom," one of the moms in my spiritual parenting group reported a few weeks after I shared my own aha. "I changed the large picture on the wall in my kids' bedroom," another mom reported. "Maybe I'm imagining it, but my sons seem to be playing more sweetly since." The new scene those kids looked at: Two boys walking hand in hand on the beach, leaving intertwined footprints in the sand.

ॐ

Actions

Create a Family Altar

My then-5-year-old daughter came bounding into the house, cheeks aglow from the outside chill, eyes blazing with the fire of joy. "Look what I found!" she squealed, holding a small, nondescript stone she'd picked up in the yard as if it were a 10-carat diamond. She immediately headed for my bedroom, to put her new treasure in the highest place of honor she could contemplate—the family altar.

Watching her push several gemstones off a little pedestal to make room for her rock, I couldn't help but smile. Although she'd hardly seemed to notice the altar and never faced it as my husband and I did while meditating (see "Try a Family Meditation"), she had clearly gotten its message: Altars are physical places that, through the thoughtfully considered objects placed on them, connect us to a higher realm. (With its evocation of Mother Earth, the rock fit right in.)

A home altar stands as a reminder that we can choose to act and react from an enlightened space all the time, not merely when in a "House of God." The carefully selected items on an altar serve as visual cues to our link to Source—a prospect all the more profound when we consider that the objects and we are all made from the same fundamental energy.

I knew of only two altars when I was a kid. There was one at my temple, where the sacred Hebrew scrolls, or *Torahs*, were stored, and another with numerous lit candles that I once saw when I accompanied a friend to Christmas Mass. Both moved me to look at them. I never contemplated the concept of bringing that spiritual touchstone into my home, though, until I became a mom. (Amusingly, I found out years later that my parents actually had Tibetan altar shelves in the house I grew up in, but since they hung them upside down and placed antique knickknacks on them, none of us knew.)

A few years after we had kids, my husband and I emptied a shelf on a bedroom wall unit (later switched to a small, low table after we moved to a larger house) and covered it with a purple cloth and some pretty scarves. Since the shelf was at eye level when we sat before it or even when lying on the bed, it turned out to be the perfect spot. The kids helped gather the objects initially placed on our altar: candles, incense, a little statue of the dancing Hindu god Nataraja given to us by a beloved yoga friend, a metal representation of the Jewish spiritual symbol of the tree of life, tiles from a recently renovated interfaith temple at a treasured spiritual retreat site, a Tibetan singing bowl, numerous gemstones carved with uplifting words, and a photo of our family. Over the years, the kids added more of their sacred additions, from a starfish and sand dollar they found at the beach to a postcard of beautiful animals, and, then, the little rock.

I loved them all. Not having grown up with the "shoulds" of an altar, I enjoyed making it up as we went along. I know I'm not the only one who does that. At a store, I once glanced through a book that featured a man's amazing car altar. All over his dashboard, steering wheel, and ceiling were objects that moved him, from a crucifix to flowers to word poems and various blown-glass shapes. Seeing that reminded me of an "altar" I had witnessed as a child (although I didn't think of it as such at the time), when my uncle's car got stuck in the mountains with five little girls in his charge and we hitched a ride to a gas station from a passing VW van. Beads, crystals, lights, nature photos, and more lined the walls inside the "peace-mobile," as they called it, which I remember soothed us frightened kids.

Years later, I came across another unique altar, this one in a multifaith women's spirituality group, where amidst the candles and chrysanthemums sat a shiny silver speculum—to celebrate our womanhood, according to the group's leader, not surprisingly a female gynecologist. Then there was the altar at a Jewish spiritual retreat, where the prayer shawl typically worn by men during services was fancifully draped on the wall behind a table filled with ceremonial candles, bread, and wine.

If you decide to create your own altar, start with a sense of unlimited possibilities. Any object displayed in a manner that evokes inspiration, wonder, awe, good memories, or Source is perfect. That's because altars aren't intended to transform a space—they are meant to transform *us*. You'll want objects that feel good when you put them in your hands. As Neale Donald Walsch writes in *Conversations With God, Book 3*, "The energy of life—what we'll call the 'Soul of God'—takes on different characteristics as it surrounds different physical objects. Indeed, that energy coalesces in a particular way to form these objects." If you want your child to feel that the altar is also hers, resist the impulse to censor her selections, although a detailed discussion at the beginning of what you hope to accomplish might keep her Army toys at bay.

Once created, your altar should be a living, breathing entity—that is, it should change whenever the mood strikes someone in your family. When a family I know had a new baby, they shifted to a "baby altar" for a time, filling their family shrine with the positive pregnancy-test stick, a lock of their newborn's hair, her birth photo, and tiny wooden blocks spelling the words "little angel." A year later, those objects had been pushed to the side to make room for the shark's teeth, Indian arrowheads, and owl feathers their older kids gathered during a wilderness expedition. Sitting on my own altar right now is a silk rose bud recently given to me by a dear friend.

What you do in front of the altar doesn't matter. Sure, it's great to meditate and chant before it, but you can get equal benefits if you and your family spend time together singing, dancing, or playing in its presence.

‿

Actions

Love Them With Your Words

There are many aspects to being an enlightened parent that I've learned in the years since I first gave birth. Some things, though, I always knew. One is to talk to and about your child as if he is the angel you know him to be.

I know that other parents also get this innately. Some name their child Grace or Star or Faith (or the names of angels, like Rafael or Gabriel). Others refer to their child with loving nouns, as does a friend who regularly alludes to her twin boys as Heaven and Treasure, a play on their names of Evan and Trevor. Regularly passing these types of words over your lips helps you view your child in the highest light, which also enhances your child's vision of himself.

In our society, though, it has somehow become okay to describe our kids in less-than-flattering terms. Unless you travel in a completely different world than I do, you've likely heard parents call their loving offsprings "bratty," "spoiled," or "trouble." Most parents say this in jest, but is their child discerning enough to realize that? And even if she is, why should that matter? If my husband called me "my annoying wife" before announcing he was kidding, he'd be sleeping on the couch all the same!

I can still recall an Academy Award acceptance speech from nearly 20 years ago because I was so shocked when I heard it. A producer who had won the coveted Best Picture honor thanked his "brilliant" head of production, his "most persevering" executive producer, his "dynamite" marketing team, his "inspirational partner and best friend," his "loving" wife, and his "beautiful" nieces. Want to know how he referred to his children? "My two rotten kids." He was obviously joking. But how must those daughters have felt hearing dad wax rhapsodic about everyone else, and then disparage the people who likely mean the most to him?

I was once conversing with a stranger in a clothing store. I was with my young daughter, so the man whipped out a picture of his own beloved child to show to me. "Here's my ugly boy," he exclaimed with a wink, handing me a photo of a 2-year-old beauty sporting sky blue eyes, porcelain skin, ringleted black hair, and ruby lips. The child wasn't with the man, but with the casual way the dad spoke this I'm sure he'd said it before and would do so again—at some point with his son in earshot. We got into a long discussion about why he hadn't said his child was gorgeous. He admitted to worrying about sounding boastful, or even jinxing the boy. I urged him to see that praising his toddler's looks could ultimately shape how the boy thinks of himself—both physically and emotionally—as he grows.

One of my favorite parenting books is *Raising Your Spirited Child* by Mary Sheedy Kurchinka. Although Kurchinka writes about children who are resistant, persistent, boundlessly energetic, or excruciatingly sensitive, she never terms them "difficult" or "problematic." To her—and to me, the mother of a persistent son to this day—they are joyfully "spirited."

When he was very young, my "spirited" son went through a stage of calling his toddler sister "stupid, dopey," whenever she would get into his toys. This angered her so she would yell back, "I am not a stupid, dopey!" I tried to tell him this was hurting her feelings, but he enjoyed the power the insult gave him. Then I had a brainstorm. If I couldn't get him to stop saying it, at least I could get her to stop accepting what she heard. The next time, I simply and quietly correct him: "She is a beautiful spirit." My daughter brightened immediately. "I am a beautiful spirit," she announced, in the tone of a royal taking her throne. Even if she didn't exactly know those words, she knew that this was what she wanted to be.

Soon, we were all referring to ourselves as beautiful spirits, including my son, who dropped the "stupid, dopey" soon after because it had lost its zing. To this day, I still sometimes tell myself I'm a beautiful spirit, especially if I'm having a bad day or things aren't going as I had intended.

Consider the power of your words whenever you refer to your child. Reflect on how you would want to be described and use similar language no matter how she is behaving in a given moment or stage. By calling her what you know she is, you may even transform a child who's been behaving in a way that might be "bratty," "spoiled," or "trouble" back to the sweetness and love that is her core. Sticks and stones may indeed break bones, but condescending names can crack both self-esteem and a child's connection with her higher self—a shattering that takes much longer to heal.

᷂

Actions

Use Reverent Tones

The contrast was so shocking it jarred me out of my bliss. I'd been eavesdropping on a conversation between a mother and a Buddhist monk, patiently awaiting my turn to speak to the spiritual guru after hearing his inspiring lecture. As is common when one speaks to a religious figure, the mom had softened her volume and sweetened her pitch, the better to reflect the awe she felt toward the learned master.

Throughout most of their exchange, her 3-year-old son sat silently on the floor. Toward the end of the conversation, he decided it would be fun to run in circles around the pair. He made an initial loop, to the visible horror of his mother (the monk seemed to enjoy the boy's energy). As he rounded the second, his mom loudly and harshly lashed at him, the sugar in her vocal cords suddenly turning to sand. "Joshua, stop that this minute!" she screamed. The boy stopped in his tracks—and I fear that the love in his heart stopped in its tracks, too, if only for that instant.

We rarely think about the tone we use—separate from the words (see "Love Them With Your Words")—when we speak to our child. Yet many of us can recall to a note a specific angry takedown our parent delivered that slashed right through us. Perhaps it was the deep timbre of disappointment. Or maybe the high shrill of rage. This is a voice that says, more powerfully than any words, "I don't respect you right now," even if it is uttered without such intent.

We all know that the tone of a voice is important. When we're on the phone with a stranger and we hear a sugar-cane intonation, we imagine the caller is beautiful and kind. Studies reveal that unpleasant pitches can affect romantic relationships: when researchers at the University of Southern California examined couples in marriage counseling, for example, they were able to accurately predict which ones would likely improve their partnerships over time based solely on the pitch, intensity, and other vocal features they used to address one another. Meanwhile, in the job market, women with creaky voices are considered less competent or hirable, Duke researchers found. Inflection even influences whether a doctor will be sued for malpractice, Tufts University scientists discovered, because those whose voice reflects less concern or more dominance have higher rates of lawsuits. And you know if you want your dog to understand that he did something awful, you make your voice stark and serious.

When my first baby was born, I found myself speaking with a sound unconsciously altered by the overflow of love from my heart. "How's my sweetheart?" I'd coo in high soprano, rather than my normally deep alto. Throughout the day until my good night (and till the second, third, and fourth good nights as he awoke continuously those first months), my voice remained elevated. I noticed that this was common, that all the moms in the "new baby" side of the playground (the area with the benches and shade trees rather than the swings and see-saws) seemed programmed to speak like angels. And why not? We were speaking to heavenly beings, after all.

But across the divide commonly known as a sandbox, older kids were talked to in an entirely different pitch. Moms with new babies *and* older kids almost sounded comical as they trilled from a gentle high octave to an abrasive low one, depending on which age child they were addressing. How could the older child not notice the contrast, I wondered. I vowed right then to keep my pitch lofty forever.

Well, like many of my vows, I found it impossible to maintain this all the time; my vocal chords didn't naturally vibrate on these upper notes. Still, as much as possible when my kids were younger, I tried to speak with a loving lilt. Sure, I sometimes lost it, shrieking, "Stop that already!" when I couldn't take something another second—although that's always a sign that I had ignored my discomfort for too long, allowing the feeling to fester and explode inappropriately rather than dealing with the issue earlier in a kinder way. Fortunately, those moments were mercifully infrequent.

My husband and I once attended a yoga retreat held in an isolated house deep in a New York forest. One evening, someone accidentally left a door open and a large bat flew in. Most of us city folks who knew bats only as extras in horror movies ducked, screamed, and covered our heads. But a woman who'd previously lived in the area and thus had something of a relationship with the native fauna stood up. She picked up a towel and walked calmly towards the frighten animal. In *sotto voce* she began telling it that she wanted to help it get back to the wild. She continued talking for several minutes, her melodic pitch calming all of us as much as it did the bat. The animal settled on a table and allowed her to place the cloth around its body and carry it outside.

Parents would do well to similarly reserve their sharp intonation only for situations fraught with immediate danger: your child running in the street without looking, chasing another kid with a stick raised over her head, obliviously racing her bicycle towards a large tree. At other times, strive to speak in a way that conveys the love that fills your heart.

"It doesn't cost anything to have loving speech," the Vietnamese Buddhist monk and poet Thich Nhat Hanh has observed, citing a verse from his spiritual tradition. Yet the loving connection it buys you and your child is pretty close to priceless.

༃

Actions

Create Community

My kids and I were doing puzzles together on the patio floor when it dawned on me: I was lonely. They were joyous companions, but I needed more (and likely so did they). My closest friend had moved far away, and like most of us in the suburbs, I barely knew my neighbors. Our family life was filled with play, work, chores, activities, and love, but we were missing a sense of belonging to a larger whole.

Generations ago, no one needed to think about community. Friends and extended families lived in the same neighborhood for decades, so everyone knew everyone. Although I'd never experienced this—and I imagine there was some claustrophobia involved, and at least an occasional wish that people weren't privy to *all* of your business—there's also something profound in knowing that your family has a place where it belongs. That there are people outside your immediate clan who cheer you during your triumphs and cherish you when times are tough. And who might treasure your child in a way that today is largely confined to his doting parents and grandparents.

You and your child can convince a neighbor that everything is fine when you simply say a cursory "hello" each evening over the sound of your closing garage door. A true community member, however, knows from the crack in your voice or the pained look behind your eyes if you're hiding a sorrow. It is only in revealing who we really are that we are fulfilled as human beings, says sociologist Brené Brown, who writes that "True belonging only happens when we present our authentic, imperfect selves to the world." I agree.

Communities are especially important sources of nourishment for kids, who thrive in knowing that everyone around them cares about them, not just their mom and dad. When I was a child, my family used to go to a bungalow colony in upstate New York every summer. The same families came back year after year, so we got to be close. It was such a thrill when another kid's parent remembered what I liked to eat for lunch or what group games I enjoyed playing. And when I fell off a monkey bar and broke my arm one wretched July day, I went to bed feeling awful but woke the next morning to a towering pile of gifts—compliments of all the families in the colony who'd joined together to boost my mood.

A community where you can share your inner life is also important for mental health, psychiatrist and author M. Scott Peck wrote in his book *The Different Drum*. "There can be no vulnerability without risk; there can be no community without vulnerability; and there can be no peace (and ultimately life) without community."

The kinship that naturally forms after years of living in the same place, working the same job, or attending the same religious organization is gone for many of us. But I have learned that, with a little effort, anyone can create meaningful community. Building such a tribe for your family involves more than surrounding yourself with a lot of people; you can be in a bustling city or a busy park and still feel alone. And it means going beyond the groups that most adults rely on for communal sustenance before we had kids (gym or yoga class buddies, 12-step meeting attendees, office pals), which may nurture us as individuals but don't do the same for our families.

Here are ways I've made community happen for my family over the years, and that could be valuable for yours:

• *Take the lead with your neighbors.* When I moved into my home a decade ago, the first thing I did was design a flyer inviting families in two dozen nearby homes to come to our house on a Sunday afternoon for pizza and cake. Over the years, this group has continued to socialize at potlucks, pool parties, moms' nights out, and sunset gatherings on someone's driveway or yard. (I compiled a list of everyone's email address that first gathering so subsequent invites were easy to distribute.) At some point during each get-together, I call the kids from their impromptu games and the adults from the food and drink tables and encourage everyone to participate in a round of out-loud sharing. This is how we learned that a neighbor got a long-desired job promotion, that another had been fired, that kids won their sports leagues (and where their games were so others could attend) or were having trouble with their homework (more than one adult has volunteered to tutor), and, sadly, that someone had been diagnosed with aggressive breast cancer (prompting a call to arms among the neighbors to drive her son to school or summer camp, among other assistance). There's nothing like knowing the people within walking distance who can take in a package and lend you eggs, or pick up and feed your kid in a pinch. And who make everyone in your family feel like they are home as soon as they enter the neighborhood. (When my car was in the shop, one neighbor even lent me hers for the week to shuttle my kids!)

• *Gather regularly with like-minded new friends.* Make a list of other young families you particularly like or with whom you share common interests and invite them over. I did this years ago with families from my alternative Jewish congregation, and it was from this group that our spiritual parenting discussion group evolved. (The adults talked while the kids played in the other room.) Worried you don't have enough space in your home? Take it outside, as I did with a different group of families that assembled for "family soccer" at a local park. Or as I also did when my kids were older and several families met every full moon for a sunset potluck at the beach. The idea is to convene regularly with the same people so everyone becomes comfortable being open and vulnerable. To help others feel that such honesty is okay, you may need to be the first to share your own fears and failures.

• *Look into cohousing.* Cohousing is a unique housing concept that combines private and communal living. Created in Denmark decades ago and brought to the U.S. by a pair of California architects (who subsequently wrote the book *Cohousing: A Contemporary Approach to Housing Ourselves)*, a typical community has families owning their homes, either apartment-style or tightly spaced houses or townhouses, while sharing a "common house" where everyone gathers. Residents hold group dinners, movie nights, football-game watching, and other events in the common house, and they play group games and sports in the shared yard. Kids in cohousing communities have been known to pass en masse from one house to another to play, eat, or sleep, since each parent knows them all. Unfortunately, with only a few dozen cohousing communities currently built in this country (Denmark has hundreds), your chances of finding one near you are small, although the number is growing. My family participated in a group trying to get one developed in

South Florida, but we ran into problems—the housing crash of 2008 didn't help—and it never happened. (It was through this effort that I learned the value of reaching out to my neighbors no matter where I lived.) Some parts of the country have several thriving communities, because when one is built and people see the benefits, they want one, too. In other areas, groups are in the early stages of working together in the hopes of creating a development that meets everyone's needs. You can find a list of built or forming communities in each state at the website Cohousing.org.

%

Actions

Avoid Competition

It was during a presidential election season when the destructive nature of competition first hit me. In the weeks leading up to the election, as I ran errands in the grocery store or mall, I noticed myself viewing other shoppers with suspicion: Were they supporting my candidate or the opponent?

The enemy—or, at least, the potential enemy—was everywhere!

For a time, my world seemed split down the middle, us vs. them, and to my mind the us's were the preferred lot. When a car drove past with a bumper sticker touting the other party, I felt disgust toward its occupants. When a neighbor I otherwise liked said he was supporting the third-party candidate, which would take a vote away from mine, my anger rose.

It took weeks before I finally got my mad-dog mind to heel. By allowing myself to get caught up in this winner-take-all mindset, I had come to see myself, my candidate, and others who voted with me as better than the chumps on the other side.

The notion of being "better than" turns out to be one of the most stubborn obstacles to enlightenment. And it is everywhere. Sign your child up for a recreational soccer league and you'll soon discover that, to many coaches and parents if not to the kids, beating the other team matters—a lot. Walk into your local elementary school and you'll see "student of the week" posters in the hall. Agree to participate in your local Girl Scout's cookie drive and suddenly you're engulfed in an insane Thin Mints-hawking rivalry.

Studies consistently find that when people or teams are pitted against one another, not only do we forget such lofty principles as "we are all one" and "what's good for me is good for you," we begin to see others as a potential obstacle to our achievement, notes educator Alfie Kohn, author of the book *No Contest: The Case Against Competition*. Research shows that students who are promised a reward if they turn out to be the best tutors of younger kids are the most likely to resent their charges if they don't learn quickly. They also view their fellow tutors with hostility, even if they'd been friends before. (Kohn's other points—that competition kills internal motivation, creativity, and the joy of doing a given task—are also noteworthy, but beyond my focus here.) Kids on the opposing soccer team, the students in your daughter's class, the other Scouts, fellow tutors—shouldn't we embrace them, not consider them to be roadblocks impeding our child's way?

To avoid situations that set our child against others, my husband and I sent our children to a non-academic preschool and later to a private Montessori elementary school—despite its considerable cost and distance from our home—because they didn't give students tests or grades. We filled our kids' closets with percussive musical instruments, including hand bells (the ultimate collaborative pursuit). We also loaded up on cooperative board games, where players work together for a common goal like bringing in the harvest before the frost or corralling all of the escaped horses. (The company Family Pastimes has a terrific line of cooperative games.)

Even traditional competitions can be made more cooperative, something I believe is especially important when kids are small and learning their place in the world. A friend's daughter's birthday party featured a newfangled version of musical chairs. I'd always hated this game, because there's a loser each round who is awkwardly left standing for everyone to see. Here, when the music stopped 10 kids squeezed onto the 9 chairs, then 10 kids squeezed into 8 chairs, then 7 chairs.... It was wonderful to watch all the kids pile onto the remaining seats and invite those still standing onto their laps, squealing as the children leaped on top of them or wiggled onto a sliver of their chair.

Even when my kids did play in competitive sports leagues (they both took to tennis and my daughter to softball when they reached elementary school), I made it a point to compare their performance to their prior level rather than to that of the other kids. "Look how easily you hit the ball," I'd say. Or, "Your backhand is really getting stronger." "I really liked how you were rooting for your teammates." I'm not saying they didn't compare themselves to others or look at the scoreboard with anticipation, but I didn't encourage that behavior.

Being a member of our ultracompetitive society, I admit I sometimes do still let divisions get the best of me (and not just during presidential elections). But when I notice myself going down the road of mentally dividing the world into I-win-you-lose, I try to stop it. It's a process I'm still working on. I'm no better or no worse at it than you.

☜

Actions

Spend Time With Elevating People

The scriptures say Jesus could spend time with everyone without lowering his lofty vibration. I admit that I'm no Jesus; I suspect few of us are. When I pass time with people who are disconnected from their higher selves, my own connection drains, too—dripping as though through a strainer until there's nothing left but coagulated goo. After an afternoon with negative people, for example, I've been more inclined to turn my back on the homeless guy on the street corner asking for money rather than to reach into my wallet for a $5 bill. I've noticed similar reactions in my children.

Life coach Cheryl Richardson categorizes low-consciousness people into several groups: The Blamers (everyone's at fault but them), the Complainers (can *nothing* in their life work the way they want it to?), the Shamers (they get their jollies putting others down), and the Gossips (trying to feel better by casting aspersions). We all have tendencies towards each of these, but it's a matter of degree.

I used to be friends with people who could be president of some of these groups. But when my vulnerable little ones came into my life, I was no longer willing to tolerate that negativity. (And, really, I shouldn't have tolerated it for myself all those years either.) I wouldn't allow a smoker to pollute my living room; why let someone emit toxic emotional fumes, which can be just as destructive?

I've always believed that people leave a bit of their energy behind when they're no longer in the room. This is partly why a deserted monastery, church, or ashram feels so peaceful, and why even an empty dance club hypes you up. A friend once told me her house felt delicious for months after her cousin's visit, during which the guest spent time meditating and doing healing work on herself. When my Aunt Jeanne passed away, I knew the person who bought her apartment was getting an even better deal than they imagined, because her loving essence undoubtedly remained in the air. Similarly, the late educator Leo Buscaglia, known as "Dr. Love" both for his passionate personality and for the course on the topic he created at the University of Southern California, used to reminisce about how the tiny, impoverished home he grew up in was so filled with his Italian family's warmth it felt more special than his neighbors' mansions.

So I began inviting people over who emanated love, to sow the seeds in our home that would encourage all of us to blossom. I had a long list of people—you undoubtedly do, also—whom I'd met at yoga centers, spiritual events, religious services, and the like. I'd previously refrained from asking them over for fear that I didn't know them well enough or that they'd think I was sloppy (with toys always scattered around) or that my food wasn't all that grand (cooking isn't my forte). But I finally realized that people connected to their higher essences aren't the type who judge.

I hosted a lovely woman from yoga several times, who came for afternoons of board games and laughter that left our whole family smiling. A couple with whom my husband and I went out to dinner was instead invited to eat at our house, so our kids could soak up their loving aura.

Equally important was limiting the visits of folks who brought us down. One woman always came over with her son so we could chat while our kids played. She was a complainer, always griping about her house, husband, finances, and even her boy. I started inviting him to come solo.

Alas, some of the most toxic people in everyone's life are family. There's a scene in the old movie *Home for the Holidays* where the main character turns to her unpleasant sister and tells her that if she were a stranger whom she met on the street, she'd toss away her phone number. The line is good for a knowing laugh, but for the sake of family unity you probably can't do that. Especially during holidays, they're going to be around. Still, there are ways to mitigate the energy drain to you and your family. You can meditate before you see them, vow to look for the aspects of them that you appreciate, limit the amount of time of your visit, and perhaps even caution your kids in advance about their character flaws so they can open up to seeing them more compassionately.

As much as possible, though, fill your home and heart with people who are kind and joyful, who see the heights your family members are capable of reaching—and who, just by being themselves, prod each of you in that same upward direction.

～

Actions

Clean a Public Loo

When I was a kid and mindlessly left books or important papers scattered around my house, I would later find them neatly stacked in my room. My grandmother lived in our home, and she loved doing good for others. As often as she could, Grandma tried to keep her generosity anonymous. Many mornings I'd go down to the kitchen for a glass of water only to return moments later to an already-made bed. (She'd never admit to having been in the room.)

Grandma routinely handed packages of her chewy, gooey chocolate-chip cookies to the mail carrier, her chiropractor, or whomever she was seeing that day. When I went away to college, she'd mail her baked sweets to my roommates and me. And she always had a ready smile and a kind word for any stranger. She knew—and taught me—the joy in doing for others. (As long as you don't overextend yourself; see "Say No Sometimes.") A simple woman without much formal education, Grandma was light-years ahead of most learned individuals in knowing that sharing fills you with appreciation, also.

I consider Grandma to be my first guru. But not being a baker and disliking making beds, when I moved away from my parents' house I wondered how to practice what I'd learned from her, especially once I experienced the time crunch of having kids. After much consideration, I chose to stake my claim in the public loo.

Years ago, I heard a story—truth or myth, I'm not sure—that when the late Swami Satchidananda (who introduced me to yoga and, indirectly, to my husband when we met at one of his lectures) wanted to get his organization recognized as a religious institution by American authorities, he had to fill out paperwork about the kinds of rituals his ministers performed. I'm sure the government was thinking marriages, baby blessings, and rites over the dead. But Satchidananda reported that his ministers always clean up the paper they find on the floor in the public restrooms they encounter.

Anonymous service at its highest and best. The kind that brings joy in the doing, without allowing your mind to seek payback. All service is spiritual, we know. The Bible asks each of us to "use whatever gift [we] have received to serve others, as faithful stewards of God's grace" (Peter 4:10). Jewish scholarship in the Talmud similarly states, "just as God clothes the naked, so shall you. Just as God visits the sick, so shall you" (Sotah 14a). I don't believe they're making it an obligation. They recognize that serving others opens our heart, allowing the love that is Source to pour through us.

I loved the swami's idea the minute I heard it—it was so reminiscent of Grandma—that I took it on as my own. Whenever I enter a public bathroom, I quietly pick up stray toilet paper and paper hand towels, using the latter to wipe any water pooled on the counter or floor. If I notice a stall is out of toilet paper, I seek out the spares and replace the roll.

When my kids were old enough to observe my actions, they

asked me why I did this. I explained that it makes my heart happy to make the bathroom cleaner for us and for the other people who will follow. Soon they began to at least occasionally pitch in.

With a small child underfoot, finding the time or opportunity for formal community service can be a challenge. Performing small acts like the one I chose is no less valuable than doing larger charitable works. As the ancient Taoist Chuang Tzu observed, "It is the wise person who sees near and far as the same, does not despise the small or value the great."

Over the years, parents have shared the little kindnesses they performed at a time when their lives were consumed by their children. If any speak to you, give them a try. When possible, do these in the presence of your child, so she can see the joy that comes from service. Should your child decide not to join in, however, honor her wishes.

• *Share your resources on-hand.* When it rains outside—as it does regularly during South Florida summers—I try to share my ultra-large, "doorman" umbrella, which I keep in my trunk, with those around me. Sometimes, that has meant running around a parking lot taking people one at a time from the store to their cars. (I did this only when my husband was in the car with the kids, or when they were old enough to sit a few minutes without me.) Other items I've shared include sunscreen at the beach, bug spray in a park, or extra water during a hot afternoon.

• *Pay vendors more than their designated fee.* If I'm having a good year financially (or, I am learning, even if I'm not), I share my good fortune by sometimes paying more than the agreed-upon fee to people who help keep my house and writing business running. It felt good, for example, to help a babysitter sock some extra money into her college fund and to know that my transcriber could more easily pay her bills. You can also leave an extra-large tip for a restaurant waiter—just because.

• *Take advantage of opportunities to donate food or money.* During the Postal Service annual canned food drive, my family loads our mailbox to the brim with rice, beans, and other staples. Similarly, at our nearby supermarket, I regularly take one of those "donate $5" coupons from the rack and add it to my total, grateful to know I'm helping a struggling family. (Don't fall into the trap of saying that charities spend too much on administration and not enough on the hungry; do it anyway, because something is always better than nothing. You can look up specific charities at CharityNavigator.org. If you desire, tackle nonprofit-organization reform when your kids get older.)

For many years, we also sponsored a young girl in Nepal through the Save the Children aid organization, with the money automatically deducted each month. Sanjita sent us photos, artwork, and the occasional letter, and we did the same, providing fun and tangible evidence that we were helping someone across the world.

• *Leave your old baby items where others can take them.* I used to give my hand-me-down kid items to charitable organizations. Then I learned they throw away a lot of the stuff because it isn't in "salable" condition for their thrift shops. To a family tight on cash and in need of a way, say, to push their two babies around, the fact that a once-pricey double stroller has a tiny crack in the footrest or some wear in the padding shouldn't negate its value. I began driving my children's old clothes and baby items to a nearby low-income apartment complex, where I'd leave the goods with a "please take" sign. I later heard most of these items were put to good use.

• *Cook a meal.* When a young mother at my children's preschool was diagnosed with a brain tumor, families got together to bring home-cooked dinners to their house, a nightly process that lasted nearly a year until she went into remission. Similar offerings occur at many churches for members going through difficult situations, or at mothers' groups for families of a newborn. You can set a ceiling for how often you can cook a meal. I found that twice a month was my limit when my kids were small.

• *Send positive energy into the world.* Sometimes, there's nothing we can actually "do" to help people in need. But we can always send loving energy their way, and our kids can do this, too. I've done it for war zones, endangered animals, and even people stuck in bad traffic, where I simply face the cars in front and beside me one at a time and beam love and patience to the frazzled drivers. Importantly, this practice—and all the others—also boosts my own feeling of contentment and calm.

༄

Actions

Unclutter Your Home

"When did we accumulate so much stuff?" I asked my husband one day in exasperation as I surveyed the shelves that had once been a showpiece for the beauty of simplicity. We had bought that walnut wall unit soon after our wedding, to have a place to store the porcelain, silver, and crystal knickknacks we got as gifts. Those items, plus our wedding photo, a graceful pewter Hanukkah menorah, and a few assorted pieces we owned at the time spread out leisurely on a unit with nearly a dozen shelves. When I walked by in those early days, I paused to take in every item.

Over the years, though, those shelves became the repository of all the things with no place to go: bowls, platters, and coasters given as hostess gifts; statues that memorialized our own or relatives' vacations; serving pieces that seemed too pretty to stow away. The beautiful menorah was now gasping for air behind six others we had somehow acquired, not to mention the assorted boxes of holiday candles. Photos of my kids through all their baby stages—and seemingly every item they ever made in arts-and-crafts classes at school—were wedged into the remaining spaces. When I walked by at that time, I ignored the items on display because so much was vying for my attention it made me woozy. What had once been an uplifting part of my home was now a depressing muddle.

What happened to that wall unit had also happened to other parts of my environment. My bedroom closet overflowed with clothes from all seasons—including boots, hats, and sweaters from long-ago winters living in New York, even though I had no cause to wear them in Florida. My kids' room looked like a toy store, and my home office was littered with books and papers for articles I'd long completed or on topics that no longer held appeal.

A moment after I acknowledged my discomfort with all this debris, I recalled a quote from Sean Penn after a fire decimated his Malibu estate, along the lines of, "If God wants my stuff so badly, he can have it." I halfheartedly desired my own conflagration so I'd be able to start again with less, the way I had when we were first married. (It's no coincidence that Hindus use the word *tapas*, which means burning, to describe the purging of emotional baggage.)

I wanted my space back. Space to once again admire my pieces. Space in my closet to better find clothes. Space in my kids' rooms for them to create. Space in my office to ponder new work. And wider spaces in the wall unit for better display.

Years before, when my friends were first married, they moved into a four-bedroom house with only enough furniture to immediately fill two of them. I loved those completely vacant rooms (which, of course, they quickly furnished). I longed for my own empty room, a room where I would never put anything, where everyone could sit or dance or roughhouse or do yoga or meditate and be at one with the void. I wanted simplicity of the mind, which I knew couldn't as easily be achieved in a house that's cluttered and cacophonous.

But getting rid of stuff when you have kids is nearly impossible. Children are the ultimate pack rats, worse than my late Uncle Ben—a man who socked away every single issue of *Fortune* and *National Geographic* magazines since his subscription started in the 1940s. Even if they no longer play with a toy, they can't part with it. After my daughter was born, for instance, my then-4-year-old son suddenly rediscovered his rattles and teething toys and wouldn't let me dispose of them. (He even claimed to adore his old toddler's basketball hoop, though he had to stoop *down* to shoot a basket.) As they both got older, my children described every item I suggested they part with as their new favorite toy.

So I came up with a plan. Each day when my kids were either out of the house or sleeping, I would remove an item, big or small, mine or my husband's, or the kids'. I would put it in the garage for a week, and if nobody looked for it, out it would go. Sometimes I had to overcome my own resistance (my ragged-looking college sweatshirt was suddenly *my* favorite), but usually I felt giddy to move them out. If the items were old and unusable, I marked them for the trash. If they were decent, I drove them to a lower-income neighborhood and gave them away. If something seemed especially useful for someone I knew, I brought it over. By taking the things out a little at a time, nobody ever missed them.

A month later, I'd purged our house of dozens of unnecessary goods. The following month, dozens more were gone. I was amazed how much we still had, but by that point most of it was loved and appreciated. In the years since, I have continued my periodic pruning, because new stuff still wanders in on an almost-daily basis.

The best part of paring down was that I created an opening for uplifting items I'd long wanted but never had a place for. I bought a statue of Kwan Yin, the Chinese goddess of mercy; two "dancing spirits" candlesticks; and an incense holder in the shape of a lotus flower. Unlike what I'd gotten rid of, these brought me joy when I looked at them.

If you're worried you won't be able to untie the string that attaches you to your stuff, know that once you begin, the lightness of being less weighted down will propel you onward. And your life, like Sean Penn's, won't be diminished at all. When you get rid of the gadgets and gizmos that don't feed your soul, you both enable your family to enjoy the newfound emptiness and to fill some of it back up with things everyone truly treasures.

꘥
Actions

Visit the Sick

When my 93-year-old great aunt fell and hurt her leg, her doctor sent her to a rehab center so she could work to regain its use. I visited her a few days into her confinement and brought my then-young daughter along. The guard at the front desk turned us away, claiming that visiting hours hadn't begun. "Anyway," he added sternly, nodding in my 4 year old's direction, "you wouldn't want her seeing some of the people in here."

The mangled limbed, the extremely aged, individuals close to death. Those were *exactly* the people I wanted her—and myself—to see. How can we know the whole spectrum of human life if we tuck ourselves away amid the picket fences, perky daffodil gardens, and smiling neighbors with fit bodies who somehow disappear when they stop smiling or lose their youth?

As a culture, we have succeeded in isolating the poor, sick, and elderly. Our understanding that there are people who need help, and our belief that we have the means to deliver it are hardly ever aroused. It's not so much that we don't have the desire, but that we don't get views of their predicaments. Most people are actually kind-hearted, as witnessed by the fact that people flock to offer money and services after a disaster is highlighted in the news. From stranded whales to those in flooded towns, once it hits the TV or a viral Facebook post, people open themselves to taking action.

This separation is true for adults, and it is even more so for kids. Society has decreed that children must be protected from the harsh realities of life, much like Prince Siddhartha's Indian family supposedly decided for him. (After he surreptitiously left his palace at age 29 and witnessed others people's decline and disease, he struggled to understand it all. Eventually, he became the Buddha.) Don't bring them to the rehab center, the hospital, the nursing home, a sick person's house, or, heaven forbid, a funeral. They might glimpse people in pain! But how can we all learn compassion if we don't see real-life ills, not just those in the news?

When my beloved grandmother lay dying in my aunt's home, I encouraged my toddler-aged son to join me in her room. Later, all 10 of her young great-grandchildren came to the funeral, turning the marking of her passing into a boisterous celebration of her life and legacy, which she would have adored. (Her elderly friends were horrified that we would expose our little ones to this rite.)

I'm not sure why people are so fearful of glimpsing the realities of life. For centuries (if not longer), people lived in multigenerational households—children watching their relatives' ills firsthand. If someone was injured—lost a foot or a leg, say—there weren't good prostheses to cover it up. Serious sickness, deformity, and death are an integral part of being human—they can strike any family at any time. We would all be in a much better position to accept this and cope if other families' afflictions happened in plainer view.

When we put ourselves and our children in the path of people who are needy or disadvantaged, we can come to know our power. Sometimes, that power can simply uplift emotions, but other times we can actually fix a situation. I once recommended a holistic doctor to a friend with an intractable condition, and after a while his treatment healed her. A man I know recently got a kidney from a total stranger when she stumbled upon his plight. A woman whose friend was dying of leukemia offered her bone marrow, which wasn't a match for the friend but turned out to be a fit for another person in the hospital, so she gave it to him.

Always, serving others serves us. When we sponsored an impoverished child in Nepal through the Save the Children organization, we not only helped the girl and others in her village; learning about the hardships in her daily life reminded us of our blessings. It's hard to complain about your shoes pinching your feet when you know of a girl who travels barefoot for miles a day to attend her school.

My daughter and I went back to the rehab center during their official visiting hours. We not only visited my great aunt, we stopped to chat with other residents, too. I suspect it made their day. I know it made my daughter's and mine.

~ə

Actions

Speak Well of Others

When my son was a toddler, my husband and I got our first glimpse that a child can be completely engrossed in his building blocks or clay-molding project and *not miss a single word* of the adult conversation going on around him. We were in the next room quietly disparaging someone we didn't like when my son looked up from his seemingly all-consuming activity and asked, "Who are you talking about?"

"Someone we shouldn't be speaking of that way," my husband replied and we swiftly changed the topic. Needless to say, we vowed to stop gossiping about this man in front of our son. And since our boy was around pretty much all of the time, we stopped talking about the guy altogether. A funny thing happened to me in the process: I began to feel better about the man. And I started feeling better about myself for not saying unpleasant things about another person.

Parents are quick to give their child life lessons about how she should ideally behave: Don't judge people for being different. If you don't have anything nice to say, don't say anything. Be kind even to people who are mean, because you don't know what they're going through.

But sometimes I noticed dissonance between these goals and my own actions. When that gap between ideal and real pops up, as it did when my son asked us that question, I realized I should try harder to adopt these goals for myself.

The offense of speaking ill of others, the one I've noticed adults are most prone to, does more than increase the chance your words will be heard by your child. The very act puts our mind in "judgment mode"— after all, we must think we're better than the person we're disparaging or we wouldn't say it. Instead of seeing their grace notes, we condemn them for the one or two traits that annoy us (in my case, the man's selfishness).

When we stop allowing our buttons to be pressed (after all, it is we who are in charge of our own reactions), we free ourselves to open to love. Once I stopped talking about the man's selfishness, I was able to see that his need for approval, no doubt stemming from his chaotic childhood, fueled this behavior. In a more compassionate frame of mind, I was more willing to meet that need directly.

People in ancient times understood the power of negative speech. "Thou shalt not curse the deaf," the Bible declares (Leviticus 19:14), an unusual proclamation since a deaf person wouldn't hear the insult. I believe this admonishment is intended for the speaker, because when we don't curse anyone, regardless of whether they can hear us, we lift ourselves to a higher plane.

So when my son entered the first grade and came home from school telling me all the bad things this boy Marc had done that day (including telling a smaller kid he could "squash her like a bug" and chiding a repairman for wearing "ugly" pants), I quelled my impulse to tell him Marc was "not a nice boy." Instead, I said, "Marc seems to want to say things that make other people sad. I wonder why he feels he needs to do that."

"Maybe Marc does it because he's scared to be in school," my son surmised (perhaps unintentionally revealing his own emotional state). We agreed that he could try to befriend Marc to help him feel less anxious. By speaking of the boy as a person in need of nurturing and by emphasizing his good traits, my son and I moved into a better place. (Until he matured a few years later, Marc continued insulting other kids, but my son no longer focused on this.)

Speaking well of people isn't something that comes easily to many of us. Gossip is a major currency of conversation, the social lubricant that propels discussions forward. If you bring up lofty principles, you'll likely get at least a few blank stares. But share some gossip and everyone jumps in.

Since we all fall into this lowly trap at least sometimes, it's wise to start small. I originally resolved to wait a minute after formulating a negative thought before allowing the words to tumble from my mouth. Occasionally after pausing I still had to speak it, but other times I was able to bite my tongue.

After a while I moved to a trickier proposition: flipping the negative statement I'd planned to say into a praise. Sometimes I have to think hard to come up with something, but I eventually always do. The rude waitress at my local pizzeria was simply trying to take my order quickly so she could deal with the overwhelming number of customers they've given her. The neighbor who never said hello was just painfully shy, a trait that helped when she'd spend hours on her artwork. That self-centered man has a generous streak when it comes to abused animals.

"Great minds discuss ideas; average minds discuss events; small minds discuss people," an old adage goes. I don't actually find anything small about talking about people. I just try to make sure that what I say about them now is generous and kind.

ॐ

Actions

Plant a Garden of Tranquility

It's been on my action list for years, but I confess I haven't yet gotten to it. Still, I have friends who've put in the time and effort and I see that the results are worth it, so I haven't given up my plan. Right outside my patio door is a small patch of grass and weeds that will make a perfect spot for a garden. Despite my best intentions, I didn't create one while my kids were young, but I'm including this action because maybe you will.

Gardens are more than pretty views or a source of delicious food. Putting nature on your doorstep is a perfect way to connect with your soul. "The earth laughs in flowers," Ralph Waldo Emerson once wrote. I would add it draws us upward via anything with roots. I think that's true whether we're actually planting a garden or just spending time in one.

Studies have confirmed the physical benefits of being near greenery. It increases happiness, reduces clinical depression, and boosts the immune system. Patients recovering from surgery in rooms overlooking nature were found to have shorter hospital stays and to need fewer painkillers than others facing a wall. You likely don't need scientists to convince you; you know how good you feel when you move beyond your computer, car, and cappuccino and get your hands in dirt.

My ideal garden—the one I've planted in my daydream and hope to some day realize in the flesh—doesn't look manicured or polished. I like the lively symphony of wild vines, ground cover, and flowers leaping in all directions. It will have a small archway or entrance gate, allowing those who enter to know they're coming into a sacred space so they can park their cares outside. Maybe I'll add a small water feature. There's something about liquid, whether it's gushing, meandering, or dripping, that feels so spiritually cleansing. Edible plants might be interspersed with fragrant ones. Although my garden will not be large given my space limitations, it will have a little path of stepping stones to remind my mind to wander; a pretty bird feeder to connect with other creatures; and a Victorian "gazing ball" (a glass orb that reflects the beauty around it). Of course, this is *my* fantasy; if your family creates a garden, it should reflect your preferences—there's no right or wrong way.

Because gardening is a spiritual pursuit, it can be addictive. I mean that in a good way. My friend started a vegetable garden some years back at the edge of his yard. Each season thereafter he converted more of his grass to garden, eventually adding a fire pit and twinkling lights to the massive plantings. Even though it's a lot of work, whenever he goes out there—or when I do—the aura of peace and tranquility quickly takes over. Maybe that's because, as the holistic physician and author Andrew Weil observes, "each garden is… a microcosm of a just and beautiful society."

The act of gardening—of getting your body under the sky and into the earth, of watching a seed or bulb transform, of ritualistically pulling weeds, of eating what you sow—is a form of meditation. This active meditation is something that can involve the whole family. Kids love planting seeds, watering plants, clearing wayward growths, and searching for worms—and their enthusiasm is contagious. The joy children have while gardening lifts us adults when we get too focused on the work to be done rather than the joy of the doing.

Even if you aren't gardening yourself, you can benefit from taking your family to a public garden, everything from community gardens to botanical ones, to nature playgrounds and parks with wild-growth sections beyond their manicured ball fields. In some cities, including my own nearby town of Delray Beach, children's gardens created specifically for kids and families are springing to life.

A while back, a friend shared with me a ritual she and her family held in their backyard paradise, a version of the Native American "vision quests" that have grounded that culture to Mother Earth for centuries. She learned it from the book *Quest: A Guide for Creating Your Own Vision Quest* by author Denise Linn, who touts these "garden quests" as ideal for suburban families. Begin by gathering stones (or twigs or pine cones) and placing them in a circle, within which each person will sit in turn. (If your children are very young, you can make the circle big enough so everyone can enter it together.) Declare your intention to have a quest on this spot, dropping all goals and agendas. One by one, each family member sits quietly in the middle, allowing nature's timeless wisdom to speak to them. Whenever they decide they've had enough, they relinquish their turn. Profound revelations may come to a participant while in the circle, Linn says, but more often the shift rises up later.

Just like the plants and flowers placed as seeds into the earth.

Actions

Act Outrageous Sometimes

Once as I was researching an article for a parenting magazine about ways to have fun with your kids, I came across a recommendation to surprise them by jumping into the tub (fully clothed) while giving them a bath. "Do you really think parents do this?" my editor asked me when I told her what I'd found. "I imagine not many," I replied chuckling. "But, really, what stops us?" she asked.

The next time I spoke with this editor, she told me she'd decided to become one of the exceptions. While washing her 3-year-old son one night, she plunged right in—work pantsuit and all! The amazed and joyful look on her child's face was worth every penny in later dry cleaning, she told me. They splashed splendidly together for a good portion of the evening, and for days afterward her son approached her with a new sense of delight. His mom had become fun!

When most of us were kids, we wore our silly antics like a badge of honor. But as adults we've convinced ourselves that we need to act properly, especially around our child. What would he think of us, we fear, if we let our hair down—or, even better, yanked it into horns above our head and painted it fuchsia?

Well, he might think that it's okay to be jolly, to find a light lining in serious situations, to maintain our childlike wonder no matter our chronological age, and to connect to other people through laughter—all wonderful life lessons we'd do well to absorb ourselves. Laugh, and the world laughs with you. What if that's not simply a line in an Ella Wheeler Wilcox poem, but also the key to surpassing our illusion of separation and exposing our united spiritual core?

When my family went one summer to a yoga camp at Satchidananda Ashram in Yogaville, Virginia, one of the practices we did was actually called "Laugh-a-Yoga." Lying on our backs, parents and children heartily guffawed for 15 minutes. The first few chuckles were forced and formal, but soon the absurdity of the practice and the unique way some people cackled brought forth genuine laughter. At the end, we felt exhilarated and more connected. As the leader of our "enlighten up" sessions put it, "Laughter bonds people. Everyone knows that when they go to a funny movie and everybody's laughing there's a great sense of camaraderie." (If you need another reason to cotton to cutting up, know that research has documented how laughter eases depression and improves oxygen flow; 100 good belly laughs have also been found to offer a cardiovascular boost similar to 10 minutes of rowing.)

After my editor's experience, I resolved to be sillier, even though by nature I'm a more serious person. My daughter was into *Pokemon* at the time, and she would sometimes pretend to fly around the house on one of the series' airborne characters. When I had to go into the kitchen or bedroom, I started asking if I could hitch a ride. She'd glide me to my destination, arms airplane-style with me "riding" behind, both of us sometimes leaping to avoid the turbulence we'd encounter. When *Harry Potter* fever later broke out in our home, I'd stop sweeping on occasion and use my broom (or stop writing and commandeer my pencil) to cast spells on the kids. Initially, I used charms from the book to lock someone's legs or make them reveal the hidden contents of their pockets. Eventually, we got to giggling and hexing one another about everything, from giving 50 kisses to making cookies magically appear on a plate.

During dinner preparation with my kids, I once announced that we were planning a feast for a prince who would be arriving soon. I also made the bed with them, squealing that we had to finish before the wicked stepfather (for equal time!) came to check our work. In these moments I stopped separating myself from the whimsical world of my children—my mature parent to their frivolous child—and met them in the place where all hearts reside.

I read about a woman who realized that rather than forcing her children to switch from one activity to another, she could join in their magical thinking. "Uh-oh, the train is coming!" she'd call to her kids who were engrossed in the park sandbox when it was time to leave. Scooping up blades of grass, she'd hand these "tickets" to her laughing children and everyone would bolt for the "train" (also known as their car).

For years, I rolled my eyes when my own dad started telling one of his jokes. But it did amaze me how he could conjure his lines about any situation. When my cousin took up piano, dad said, "I know a boy who made money from his piano; his neighbor paid him weekly not to play it!" When I bought new shoes, dad told his yarn about a little kid whose mom told him his shoes were on the wrong feet. "No they're not, Mom," he replied. "I *know* they're my feet."

Well in his eighties, my dad is as vibrant and healthy as a man half his age—a fact I now attribute to his desire to see the world with a wink and a smile, and to share that twinkle with everyone around him. So when my daughter asked me one year what I was going to be for Halloween trick-or-treating, I resisted my impulse to tell her that dressing up was just for kids. We went out that year as the goofiest pair of mother-daughter puffy pumpkins anyone has ever seen.

༄

Actions

Try a Family Meditation

As dawn breaks, the whole family sits around the altar, each silently focusing on the breath—in and out, in and out—during our daily ritual of meditation. The smell of incense wafts gently through the room. It is stone silent, everyone in too deep a meditation to utter a peep or move a muscle. We each experience the absolute bliss that comes from losing oneself in intense focus, especially in the presence of people we love.

In my dreams!

That may have been my fantasy for our family meditations, but it certainly has never been our reality. Sitting meditations—the act of being still and focused on one thing until your mind stops leaping, allowing you to merge with your higher self—is tough enough for adults; for most kids, it's near impossible. This is why I consciously labeled this chapter with the word "try." A good meditation—even if it lasts just a few seconds—can be so wonderful that it's worth seeing how it goes with your family. But if it isn't fun or you can't pull it off, don't sweat it. Maybe try again when your child gets a little older.

Despite my own love of daily meditation, at its height we only got around to meditating as a family maybe once a week. That was when my children were little; when they got older, instead of sitting more they decided to stop joining us altogether. (Regardless, my husband and I still sat daily.) Even when we did meditate as a group, my son typically got antsy and left the room after a few minutes. My daughter stayed mostly because she wanted to lead the Sanskrit chanting we ended the session with. She fidgeted a lot during the silent sitting, displaying her impatience with the whole ordeal.

Still my husband and I continued to invite them. We've long believed that most of the gains from meditation come from simply showing up, an act that tells the brain it's the soul's time now, even if the brain resists stepping aside. The benefits of just a few minutes of meditation can be felt immediately. As the spiritual teacher Esther Hicks explains in her book *Ask and It Is Given*, "When you quiet your mind, you offer no thought; and when you do so…the vibration of your Being is high and fast and pure."

Why bother to meditate with kids in the house? Precisely because you have kids in the house. Parents benefit from the reduced stress, enhanced clarity, improved mindfulness, and increased sense of love that even a "mediocre" meditation delivers. In addition to their potentially heightened connection with Source, kids gain from seeing that you believe meditation is an important practice, one they may eventually come to appreciate and perhaps adore.

In our culture, meditation is frequently intertwined with prayer, because both involve reaching for Source. But typically when we pray, we engage our mind to offer gratitude or to ask for what we need. "Thank you for the bountiful food." "Please take care of Uncle Harry." "Please let me get that gift for the holidays." In meditation, our aim is to make our mind clear and blank, asking for nothing but the ability to be one with the moment and the world. Or, as the authors of the *Whole Parenting Guide* put it, "In prayer we speak and God or the universe—we fervently hope—listens. In meditation, God or the universe speaks, and we listen." By guiding ourselves beyond our mind, we can eventually come to see that we are not that mind, or our body, but rather the gentle stillness underneath them.

With a regular practice, we can train our mind to focus on one thought or action, an improved concentration we carry with us the rest of our day. My daily meditation used to help me keep my mind from wandering when my son would describe, in the most minute detail, the video game he'd just played. Since it meant the world to him, I wanted to pay attention, even if I found it a challenge.

You can begin your family meditation any way you want. (Like me, you might also sit solo at a different time of the day, to go more deeply.) A woman I know entices her kids to meditate as part of a larger morning ritual in which she reads them a spiritual story, they do a bit of yoga, sing an uplifting song, and then sit together for a few minutes of silence. Another family gets the kids to come by placing an "offering" of cookies on the altar (See "Create a Family Altar"), a treat the universe shares with her children after the silence. I believe this is preferable to dragging screaming kids to your session, but I'd rather let the meditation be its own reward. Some kids will never take to it, but others eventually enjoy stilling their wild minds and feeling a connection with something larger than life.

I like to sit on the floor in front of my altar, but you can meditate anywhere that feels peaceful. We begin our practice with Sanskrit chanting, which the minute I open my mouth clears the cobwebs that have taken root in my brain. Give each member of the family, including your child, a chance to start a round of chanting, which the others repeat responsively. One line is typically repeated many times so they're easy to learn. You can find sample chants online, although I suspect you could benefit just as much by singing any uplifting tune in any language.

Then comes the time to be quiet. Everyone sits erectly (you can place a pillow under your butt and/or lean against a wall to help your back), palms resting lightly on the thighs, eyes closed, the breath coming in and out delicately through the nose. The lights should be dimmed or, in daylight, off entirely. Invariably, a long-lost cousin will call right at this moment, which is why it's critical for everyone to turn off their phones.

The most common form of meditation is a focus on the breath. Breathe in to a silent count of four with long, slow breaths originating deep in the diaphragm. Then breathe out to another count of four, and so on. The Hindus call the natural desire of your brain to jump from one thought to another "monkey mind," and all of us have it. Getting it to relax for just a few seconds in the beginning is fantastic. Typically, by the time you get to count three of the first inhalation your mind is already running elsewhere. (Onto how your legs are getting cramped, or did you leave the teapot on the stove to burn, or where is the form you have to sign for your kids' school, or, inevitably, how proud you are that you're doing so great in this meditation.) Observe your mind's escape without judging, and bring it back to your breath each time. Set your timer the first few sessions for just two or three minutes, ideally building from there. The longer you sit, the more you train that monkey mind to heel.

Although the breathing meditation is the simplest (note I didn't say "easiest"; it isn't easy to calm an active mind, especially with a child in the room), your family may prefer another method. Candle gazing involves placing a lit candle in the center of the floor (obviously, this is a non-starter if your kids are young enough to knock it over) and staring at the flickering flame—eyes half-closed to minimize distracting stimuli. Mantra meditation is saying a word or syllable silently or aloud over and over. You can use English words like "love," "peace," or "harmony" or a common Sanskrit phrase such as "Om" or "So-ham." (In our family meditations, we spent a few minutes silently counting breath and then a few minutes saying a mantra together out loud. I think sound helps young children to focus.) There's even a walking meditation, good for kids who can't sit still, which involves taking slow, deliberate steps (about one step every five seconds), with eyes cast down, hands clasped behind the back, and your gaze on the space where the prior person just left an invisible footprint.

Regardless of the type of meditation, end each session with a moment that solidifies its sacredness before everyone makes their mad scramble to the kitchen or the phone. In our home, we'd stand in a circle and hold hands, "squeezing" a bit of love into the hand of the person to our right, until the love goes around a few times. Then we put our hands together into prayer position and bow to the light inside one another.

We accompanied our bows with the Sanskrit word "Namaste" which means "I salute the divine essence within you." For a long time, our children thought my husband and I were saying, "Have a nice day," so that's what they repeated back to us—an equally lovely sentiment with which to move on to our next activity.

ॐ
Actions

Thank Source, Often and Out Loud

"Thank you, Source, for the kid who accidentally erased my son's saved video game after many hours of hard play. Thanks, too, for my daughter's clinging onto me, which keeps me from going to the mailbox unfettered. And thanks for the jar of salsa I broke on the kitchen floor."

"Huh?" my husband asked after overhearing my prayers of gratitude that day.

I couldn't blame him for being skeptical. In truth, so was I. But I had just read a unique passage on gratitude in a spiritual book and thought I should give it a whirl.

I often expressed thanks to Source for all the wonderful things in my life, knowing that this is a crucial spiritual practice. Anytime I can recognize and therefore focus on a blessing, it connects me with my higher self, which always sees those things. But this gratitude exercise talked about going beyond positive events to appreciate everything, because even bad experiences can have wonderful side benefits if we look for them.

Saying thanks for the erasure of my son's electronic efforts, for example, focused my mind on my son's response, which was not to throttle one of his friends (as he may have wanted internally), but to more maturely share how upset he was yet to let the boy know he was still welcome at his home. Seeing the good in my daughter's attachment took a few minutes, but I eventually realized I should better enjoy our time together, since I already knew from her older brother that all kids eventually pull away. And that salsa? It forced me to rethink my dinner menu, allowing me to make a delicious recipe I'd discovered a while back but never got to trying.

Sarah Ban Breathnach, author of the book *Simple Abundance*, once wrote that expressing appreciation changed the way she viewed her finances, regardless of the number she saw in her checkbook. "When I looked at my life's ledger, I realized I was a very rich woman," she observed. "I came to an inner awareness that my personal net worth couldn't possibly be determined by the size of my checking account balance." By shifting her quest for financial security into one for "financial serenity" she felt more at peace, and, as often happens when we align ourselves with Source, more money followed.

Some years back, an Olympic gold medal swimmer spoke about her earlier effort to attend the Games, but she didn't qualify for the team. That failure was a good thing, she reflected, because it enabled her to focus on her life outside swimming that she had previously ignored. It also made her realize how much she wanted this accomplishment, propelling her to train harder and ultimately to fulfill her Olympic dream. Some people who have survived cancer say the same: What might be considered a tragedy was, in retrospect, a gift, because of how it shifted the next phase of their life.

Better to look for those positives in the moment of a "bad" thing's occurrence, I decided, rather than having to wait years or decades for that aha. So I began adding those thanks for unwanted aspects. The dirty dishes in the sink became an opportunity to appreciate all the wonderful food we have to put on them; broken eyeglasses a chance to buy something new and trendy; my daughter forgetting an afternoon softball practice more time to read books together. Recently, my recovery from several years of digestive woes has brought me an appreciation for every delicious meal I now put in my mouth.

Saying thanks for at least some aspect of what's going on in our family—the good, the bad, and the incredibly ugly—reminds us to seek out the silver lining amid the storm that is parenting. I'm also convinced that expressing the appreciation out loud encourages our child to think that way about her own challenges.

Visual cues help me remember to do this, similar to the way religious Jews put *mezzuzot*, or scrolls of parchment in decorative cases, on the doorframes of each room as their own reminder of Source. I placed cards from decks of well-being quotes by Esther Hicks and Eckhart Tolle around my home. Whenever I walk by and read one, I prompt myself to ponder if there's anything troubling in my life that I can view differently. With a little thought, I always come up with at least one benefit. This has been an incredibly powerful spiritual practice, for which I thank Source—often, and out loud.

Nourish Yourself

"Nothing has a stronger influence psychologically on their environment and especially on their children than the unlived life of the parent."
—Carl Jung

Nourish Yourself

Wake Up and Inhale

It was the only five minutes I had completely to myself when my kids were little: The time after I'd woken up in the morning but before anyone else knew, so I could be sure I wouldn't be interrupted. For years I squandered that time by jumping out of bed and into the bathroom. Then I realized I could use those moments wisely, to set myself up for an enlightened day.

Breathwork has long been a beloved practice for calming my mind and centering myself. I'd originally learned about these conscious breathing exercises in my yoga classes. (*Pranayama*, as it is called in the yoga tradition, typically precedes or follows the poses.) When my children came along and my time for yoga contracted, I spent less time on this marvelous activity.

Then, in short order, I read an article by holistic doctor Andrew Weil touting the benefits of even a few minutes of breathwork; I interviewed Gay Hendricks, the author of the book *Conscious Breathing*, for a magazine article and he told me conscious breathing is directly correlated with a conscious life; and I ran across an adorable T-shirt that read, "Breathe slow, live long." (This quickly became part of my wardrobe.) I was clearly getting the message that I should take more time to inhale.

I began looking for avenues where I could squeeze breathing exercises into my day. It proved harder than I imagined. Once the day got roaring, it seemed to propel itself full-tilt until nightfall. By the time the kids drifted off, I was usually too tired to focus. That's when I realized those first-morning minutes were my golden opportunity.

Most breathing practices can be done lying down (although books typically suggest sitting up because when you're supine you can accidentally doze). I started to do them in bed with my eyes closed and my body still, so even if my kids were sleeping in my bed (as they often did), they wouldn't know I was up. I knew that if they realized during those minutes that I was awake, they'd leap on me as surely as a snake eyeing a rat for supper.

Once I regularly incorporated this practice into my morning, I stumbled on another advantage of doing it first thing: It shifted my mood for the entire day. When I spend those few minutes—even today, when my kids are no longer in the house—watching my breathing, I am remarkably calm. That calm carried me the morning I woke to my toddler's having spilled paint all over the kitchen table, or when my son informed me he'd lost the directions to his field trip as we were heading out the door.

Somehow, being aware of our breath, and perhaps enticing it to come from deep in the abdomen, causes it to work its magic even hours later. Religious Hindus know this, which is why they practice breathwork at dawn. I never could crack my eyes open quite that early, but I've found that doing it any time I first arise works wonders. Researchers have even documented some of breathwork's effects, noting that our typically shallow chest breathing increases muscle tension, speeds up our heart rate, and heightens our reaction to stressful events more than deeper respiration does.

I once read that yoga masters test their enlightenment by striving to observe on awakening whether their first conscious breath is an inhalation or an exhalation. I began my practice with this "first breath awareness." (It's harder than it seems. By the time your groggy mind remembers you want to do this, you've probably taken at least a dozen awake breaths already.) Then I'd move to focusing on a few of those inhalations and exhalations without trying to change them in any way. If I'd had a scrumptious night's sleep (a rarity for most parents), I'd observe that my breath was long and feathery. Other times, like when I'd wake from an unpleasant dream, it was short and quick. Tracking the breath for a few cycles helped me attune to this link to the world of spirit that is always literally right under our nose. Our breath is the most concrete way Source "talks" to us each day, and focusing on its natural flow is a wonderful way to hear it.

I followed that awareness with deep abdominal breathing, which takes oxygen down into the torso, not just into the upper chest. This abdominal breathing is what babies and toddlers do naturally, so if you've got one in the house watch his belly rise and fall sometime while he's sleeping. If you're not already on your back when you first wake up, you'll need to stealthily turn over to do this, relaxing your arms and legs into the "corpse pose."

You begin by inhaling through the nose as slowly and finely as you can, filling the abdomen with air so it rises like a balloon. Once the abdomen is full, continue inhaling until the lungs fill up to the shoulder blades. If you can, do this inhalation to a slow count of eight, but if that's too hard do whatever's comfortable and build from there. When you are ready, exhale equally slowly and finely, reversing the order so the air is expelled out the nose from the upper and middle chest before contracting the abdomen.

After a couple of minutes (longer if you have that luxury), move on to your final practice, the "healing light breath." Remain in the corpse position and gently move your hands to your upper abdomen, the location of the spiritual *chakra* called the solar plexus. With each slow, deep breath, imagine a golden light is entering through your nose and moving into your lungs and solar plexus. As you exhale, visualize the light flowing to all parts of your body—down to your toes, out to your fingers, around your torso, and up through your head. Envision that this is Source's love flowing to and speaking with all the cells in your body.

After these few moments, you can alert your child that you are no longer sleeping. Embrace her in a morning hug while seeing that golden light leap from your body to hers. This entire practice takes just a few minutes, but I promise the shift in how you'll parent your child that day will last infinitely longer.

Nourish Yourself

Anoint Yourself Each Morning

When my kids were young, I flew to New York for a brief business trip. I decided to stay with my longtime friend (and I mean *longtime*; we met when I was three), a single woman with a big apartment in the heart of the city. Although she lived on the ninth floor of a doorman building, the inside of her place seemed similar to my suburban home.

Except for the bathroom.

Where my shower held a bar of Ivory and some bargain shampoo, hers was a cornucopia of fruity soaps, hair lotions, and body gels, plus loofah sponges to apply them with. My makeup was housed in a chipped plastic container; hers in an elegant brass basket. And the brushes! A hair and blush brush for me, at least a dozen assorted shapes and sizes for her. I spent extra time in that bathroom during that trip, and when I emerged from the room I felt like royalty. It's amazing what a little lavender and lilac can do.

By the time I got home a few days later, I realized that it wasn't the specific items that brought out the queen in me. The boost came from the act of pampering myself, which, as Jennifer Aniston says in those L'Oreal commercials, conveys the message that "I'm worth it."

Back home with my two kids, I couldn't spare the time to put on the stuff in her bathroom. Nor did I want to spend all that money. But I was certain I could work that mood magic by adding a few uplifting minutes to my morning routine. It never ceases to amaze me how the exact same act performed with an altered attitude brings on a completely different experience. Yet it happens all the time. Think of how you feel cleaning up a big mess after your child's joyful birthday party versus the mess when he angrily shakes out his toy box onto the floor. Or when you wake up early because you're catching a flight for vacation compared with rising that same hour to sit in rush-hour traffic to work. I remember taking a yoga class where the instructor counseled everyone to turn their head while lying on the mat "as if an angel were putting her hands on your cheekbones and delicately guiding it to the other side." I'd never experienced such bliss simply by shifting positions.

A few weeks before my New York trip, I'd watched a public television special on the coronation of an ancient king. As part of the ceremony, the king was anointed with holy oil before his jeweled crown was lovingly placed on his head. I, too, could anoint myself each morning—albeit with shampoo—as a way of declaring my worth to myself. I actually used to do a variation on this ritual when I was a teen, brushing my long, silky hair a hundred strokes each night, honoring that which I felt was serving me.

I went to my local health-food store and picked up a deliciously scented natural shampoo and body wash. The next morning, during the few minutes allotted in my schedule to get myself ready, I gave my experiment a try. It was so successful, it's a practice I still do many mornings all these years later.

I begin by imagining myself to be Cleopatra entering her royal bathing room. I glide into my shower, then envision the basic city water flowing through the pipe transforming into energized crystalline liquid dancing off a waterfall and onto my body. I wash my hair with the floral shampoo, using the care of one preparing a princess to meet her subjects. Similar homage goes into cleansing my body. There's a custom in the Jewish tradition where people say a blessing while they wash their hands. I'd tried this a few times years before, but found the experience sterile. Then I attended a Jewish spiritual retreat where we were instructed to drizzle water from a pitcher over our individual fingers, each time envisioning a quality or memory we wished to wash away. In the shower, I feel the water similarly discarding anything I don't desire. After my shower, I towel dry my skin with reverence (the way I used to dry my babies after their baths).

Sometimes I'll even sing while I'm in the shower. I knew a really sweet man who lived to be 99 years old who attributed his health, longevity, and happy outlook to his belting out "Oh What a Beautiful Morning" as he bathed each day. Sometimes I'll sing Bob's song, but I also enjoy others, especially Natasha Bedingfield's "Unwrittten" with the line, "Live your life with arms wide open."

Anointing yourself in the bathroom is not an egotistical act. It's a statement to yourself about your value, and a way to connect with your inner magnificence so you can share that magnificence with those around you. In her book *A Return to Love*, spiritual author Marianne Williamson writes of our individual greatness and the power we tap into when we let it shine through. "We ask ourselves, who am I to be brilliant, gorgeous, talented, and fabulous?" she declares. "Actually, who are you not to be? You are a child of God..... As we let our own light shine, we unconsciously give other people permission to do the same."

Putting on my clothes the first morning I elevated my bathroom ritual in those extra minutes, I perceived a different person smiling back in the mirror. It was the face of a woman eager to share my grace with everyone whose life I would touch that day, including my children. I walked out of the bathroom and spotted my daughter, her clothes in hand, waiting as usual for me to help her dress. Filled with my own sense of value—a feeling overworked parents can so easily lose touch with—I was honored to serve.

Nourish Yourself

Choose Your Food With Care

Balancing your child's needs with those of your own is as delicate a task as steadying a rose petal on a pin top. It's easiest to give in to your child's all-consuming desires and just let the petal plop to the floor. Nowhere is that more true than in the arena of food.

We know our body would prefer a lunch of dark leafy greens topped with crisp yellow peppers, deep red tomatoes, curly purple cabbage, exotic mushrooms, ruby red beets, and a handful of pea sprouts, plus some cashews or grilled chicken or hard boiled eggs. But on most days we instead give in to our child's demand for a cheese sandwich *right now*, filling ourselves with her leftover crusts.

Sure, a parent can make it through the day on powdered macaroni and cheese and cold pizza, but by doing so you short-change yourself and your child. Fortunately, giving our body the fuel it needs doesn't have to be complicated, time-consuming, or expensive. It merely requires moving faster through the middle aisles of the supermarket where the processed items abound and spending more time at the outer edges, where fresh fruits, vegetables, lean meats, nuts, and eggs reside.

Whole foods filled with all the fiber, nutrients, and vital energy that nature intended for us were once the only things anyone ate. But because of their living enzymes, they spoil quickly and are unable to languish in the supermarket for weeks or months. When machines for processing out these enzymes became available early last century, it's no wonder stores and consumers snapped up these more convenient foods. When companies strip all the sustenance out of food, though, even when they try to put some of it back in the form of fortification, much is lost.

Our bodies intuitively know this. Think back to the last time you had, say, a bowl of steaming steel-cut oatmeal topped with your favorite fruits, nuts, and spices (mine are blueberries, almonds, dates, and cinnamon). A bed and breakfast my husband and I went to more than a decade ago in northwest Connecticut featured this exact morning fare. For months after we came home I kept dreaming of going back. I tried to figure out what was most enticing: The gorgeous countryside? The friendly inn owners? The smell of the crackling fireplace in the winter air? Yes, yes, and yes. But what I most missed was that breakfast. It was not only delicious, it was so much more sustaining than the tea and toast I usually grabbed while my kids were momentarily occupied. Fresh, whole foods nourish all our cells, which connect us to the living energy of the earth and help us parent at our best.

If you're not yet convinced that eating well yourself is important, know that if you improve your own eating habits your kids' habits may get better, also. Studies have shown, for instance, that repeatedly exposing your child to a food he does not like may lead him to eventually enjoy it. I'm not saying he'll automatically dive into vegetable stir fry when he really wants fried chicken and French fries. But there are plenty of ways you can add more vegetables and fruits and reduce the sugar and carbs (and switch the grains you do use from refined to whole) that will go down smoothly for everyone.

No matter how hectic your morning is, pick one day next week and start it with a bowl of hot oats, amaranth, or quinoa. You can make a large batch the night before and heat some up in the morning, topping it with whatever fruits and nuts you enjoy. Eat it slowly and mindfully, savoring each bite and appreciating every nutrient your body will absorb. Or make an omelet of eggs and vegetables, or forgo the idea of breakfast foods altogether and make a morning salad, like the Israelis do. Later, for dinner, fill your plate with lots of lightly steamed or sautéed vegetables and use the rice or pasta that may have previously been the star as a small side.

If you've never met a vegetable you've liked, that just means you haven't experimented widely enough. Most of us have fallen victim to the same rotation of broccoli, string beans, spinach, and corn that we grew up with, when there are actually thousands of options.

Having been a vegetarian in my twenties, I'd thought I was pretty familiar with most types of veggies. But when I moved to Florida I subscribed to a community supported agriculture (CSA) farm a few hours up the state that shipped organic produce once a week directly to my door. These vegetables (arriving a day after being plucked from the ground) not only tasted amazing, each box contained at least one item I'd never heard of before. Lambsquarters? (A cousin of spinach that was as striking to look at as it was to eat.) Mizuna greens? (The feathery leaves added texture as well as taste to my salads.) Purple cauliflower? (The better to make a colorful sautée.) You may be able to find a similar option to get fresh exotic produce delivered. (CSAs have become more prevalent in recent years, so I now buy from an even closer farm.) If you look in the nooks of your supermarket's produce section or head to a local green market, you're also bound to discover unusual fare.

The key when planning your recipes is to think "whole." Whole foods fill your whole being—body and soul. After a lunch of black beans and veggies over a little brown rice (for convenience, you can use quick rice and canned beans), you'll feel revitalized. Ditto after eating a plate of roasted vegetables (they take a while to cook, but preparation is quick). And once you get used to the nutty taste of dense peasant bread (not the overly milled white or even whole grain loafs in the bread aisle), you'll wonder why you ever gave your body the flimsy stuff.

The truth is that cooking fresh food doesn't even have to be more time-consuming than heating prepackaged fare. I have a one-pot recipe that was a staple when my kids were small, where I start boiling soba noodles (Japanese buckwheat noodles, which you can find in many regular supermarkets), and when I have five minutes left I dump kale, collard greens, green beans, tofu squares and seaweed into the same pot. After I drain everything, I add a few tablespoons of sesame oil and tamari and a sprinkling of sesame seeds and we're good to go. Many recipes found online that feature fresh vegetables are ready in the same 20 minutes frozen pizza requires.

Eating well is not a luxury you should bestow upon yourself on the rare occasion you get to eat without your child. It should be a daily affair, as important as brushing your teeth—but oh so much tastier.

@

Nourish Yourself

Spend Time Emotionally Refueling

I went out by myself one Saturday, when my second child was very young. Not to attend a business meeting. Not to tackle the grocery store, nor to buy that gift for my friend's daughter's first birthday party. Not even to bring a casserole to a woman who'd been ill. I spent an entire afternoon at a spa.

Anyone with a small child will immediately recognize the subversiveness of such an act. And it certainly was for me, a mother who had hardly gone anywhere non-work-related without a kid (including the bathroom!) in years. In fact, when I mentioned my decadent afternoon to a good friend, she asked me if I was feeling okay, figuring I must have been acting on a doctor's orders.

The only orders I'd been acting on were my soul's. Okay, maybe my loving husband's, too. He'd bought me a gift certificate for this spa for our anniversary months earlier. Although I had fantasized many times about being pampered there, I hadn't felt entitled to leave my baby for so many hours. My husband kept pressing, and finally I couldn't find a reason to keep procrastinating.

The experience was sublime. I'm convinced that spas were invented by someone in the throes of inspiration from Source. An hour full-body massage, where knots slipped from my sore muscles like butter dripping off a slice of hot toast; a jasmine-and-vanilla herbal wrap, which at first felt like I was entombed in sweaty blankets but quickly morphed into a snugly, fragrant cocoon; time in the whirlpool and steam bath to purge my skin and my emotions; and fresh fruit to nibble on between bodily treats that, for once, I didn't have to wash, peel, or cut myself.

Here's my major confession: In the hours I was at that spa I did not once think about my children.

It was only as I walked out the spa door that I was seized with a vision of my angels standing by the window, lovingly and patiently awaiting me at home. Okay, more likely they were tearing the house apart, leaving dishes all over the kitchen and toys all over the floor. But viewing their cherubic side was easier now that I felt coddled and uplifted.

Parents—especially mothers—so easily justify not spending time on ourselves. We're too busy doing things for others, we say. Mostly, I wouldn't have it any other way. But from that spa experience I came to understand that if I don't give myself a little time for personal pleasure, I have less of the good stuff to give everyone else. The heart first feeds itself life-affirming blood before pumping the rest out to the body. Parents must come to see the wisdom of doing the same.

When we embrace our moment of joy or solitude (which can be experienced in a spa full of people), we recharge our batteries. And as we tap into the peaceful vibration that bubbles up during these endeavors, we are better equipped to later respond to even the most trying parental moments with ease.

Spending a few minutes alone is also important. This can be a challenge, I know, because we place our child's and our partner's needs high on our agenda, and those needs require an incredible amount of time when our child is young. But, really, how long does it take to sneak in 15 minutes of true me-time? (Downing a pint of ice cream in front of the TV after a rough day or sweeping the floor while your baby naps doesn't count.) Treating yourself to a few-minute meditation grabbed before bed or a moment listening to chanting music or joyful jazz is not a selfish act. Neither is going off for an occasional afternoon at a spa.

"Me" time can be about rest—meditation, yoga, standing still in a rain shower.... Or you can partake in an activity that brings you joy—writing something, learning to play the flute, gardening, doing carpentry work, painting, hiking, or even shopping for something you treasure. It helps if you minimize conversations with others that take you out of yourself.

One week after my spa adventure I ventured out by myself again, this time to a women's spiritual discussion group I'd long wanted to attend. As I was sitting in meditation with this room full of women on a similar spiritual path, I felt my entire being lift. It didn't seem self-indulgent anymore; it felt as necessary to good parenting as getting a night's sleep.

Don't simply ponder actions that nourish your soul, like I did about that spa for all those months. Take at least a few minutes each day and several hours each week to turn those aspirations into action, that longing into activities that feed your self-love.

Nourish Yourself

Say No Sometimes

Want to chair that luncheon for the PTA? Bring snacks to your daughter's Scouting outing? Chaperone your son's school field trip? Have your child participate in a made-from-scratch Halloween costume parade? Attend a cocktail fundraiser organized by a former coworker? Babysit your neighbor's kids?

Me neither. At least not all of the time.

Sure, it feels good to say yes when asked, especially if, like me, you're the type of person who gets pleasure from making people happy. There's nothing like the look on their faces when I've done something they've asked me to. Maybe you know the feeling.

But sometimes when others make requests, we too easily let our lips say yes while our mind is screaming, No way! Oprah Winfrey calls it "the disease to please," and it's an ailment she herself suffered much of her life. Yes, she'll give money to this charity because you asked. Sure, she'll attend that event to help it be a success. Yup, she'll make that call you need her to. Ultimately, the constant giving exhausted her. (And Oprah doesn't even have kids!) She began to feel depleted and her generosity abused, so she vowed, she wrote in her magazine at the time, "to never again do anything for anyone that I do not feel directly from my heart."

When you have a child, so much of your time is spent keeping up with the needs of your family and home. The free minutes that remain must be seen as the precious commodity they are, to be filled with at least some activities you, too, feel directly from your heart.

Don't get me wrong; I'm all for good causes. If helping injured animals is something that calls to you, by all means agree to go with your work colleague to the shelter. If your best friend's son has a congenital disease and she asks you to assist with her fundraiser, do it with gusto. But with free time so tight, don't get caught up volunteering for things that feel like chores, even if they are objectively worthwhile. It's too easy to lose yourself to the swirl of these events, and, by extension, to the whirlwind that can become your life.

Look back on your past month. Did you agree to cook your signature dish for a Saturday charity event even though you had to miss something you preferred to do at that time? Acquiesce to a relatives' request to host a big holiday dinner even though you wanted to hold a quiet family picnic at the lake? Attend a fundraiser simply because someone requested it? If you volunteered to do anything you didn't desire—something that ate into your time, made you feel unappreciated, or didn't excite or satisfy you—ask yourself why you did it. And try to keep from doing it again.

Psychologists posit that most of us fall victim to this yes-mess because we think people will care more about us if we comply. But you have to care more about yourself, at least more than you may do now. When I agreed to make my signature dish, a black-bean-and-spinach lasagna, for that Saturday event, I knew the only hour

I'd have to cook it was the morning of the picnic—the day I usually snuck off to yoga class. Sure I got a charge watching people enjoy my food and raising money for a wonderful organization, but in retrospect I wished I'd asked if I could bring over a ready-made item instead.

How do you say no if the word gets stuck in your throat? When you understand that doing what's best for you is as important as doing for others. Sure, there are good causes. But they're *other people's* causes. I was once asked to stand in the mall with a friend on a holiday Monday raising money for injured birds. I like birds well enough, but that's not my passion. I decided it would be better if I wrote a check and let her fill my place with someone more devoted, who would probably be a more impassioned spokesperson. Remember, too, that anything you do begrudgingly or without sufficient time you probably don't do well. I remember hearing about a woman who chronically overcommitted because she wanted everyone's approval, which caused her to deliver everything later than she promised. "Sorry" became her most uttered word, and most likely this negated her sought-after appreciation.

Psychologists say that at the heart of being able to say no is knowing that you and your priorities matter. While I was writing this book and my prior one, I said no plenty, because even pleasurable activities like going out for dinner with friends or attending a fundraiser would keep me from creatively expressing what wanted to emerge. My no's were always accompanied by gratitude for having been asked (and, sometimes, a donation to the cause), but they were unshakable.

Begin slowly, by saying no to a few things you least enjoy and expand from there. Some people suggest practicing saying no in front of a mirror or telling someone you'll get back to them if you can't say no in the moment (then get back with a pleasant decline, by text or email if you find it hard to communicate directly). Avoid drama and justifications by saying simply, "I'm so sorry, I can't," and leave it at that.

If you think you're not allowed to refuse because you've got nothing else scheduled for that time, know that "doing nothing" is a crucial spiritual practice. Society disparages down time, but those moments when you allow yourself to *be* help you ponder what most excites you—an inner knowing that ultimately best guides you to the requests where you can honestly give a passionate and full-throated, "Yes I can!"

◉

Nourish Yourself

Carve Out a Sacred Space

My sister and her husband moved into a new house just before their first child was born. There was a little room off the kitchen—a nook, really, not even a complete room. It was too small to be a home office and too visible to be for storage. They decided to make it my sister's sitting room. The idea took hold that she would bring in her rocking chair and an oversized throw and put her feet up with a good book and cup of hot tea while the baby napped.

It was a wonderful plan, but one that immediately fell victim to the reality of a newborn. (I think every parent has a story of the pre-baby vision that went kaput after the birth. Journalist Maria Shriver reportedly had aimed to keep anchoring the Saturday news from New York and the Sunday morning show from Washington, D.C., all while living in Los Angeles. When her baby came, an exhausted Shriver quickly ditched both weekend gigs.) My sister never claimed ownership of the room—never put her feet up, never drank the tea. Her baby was born and her rocking chair was hauled to the nursery for those middle-of-the-night wakings. The myriad infant gear that quickly followed her daughter's debut—swing, bouncy seat, baby gym, activity center, jumper, and more—found a perfect home in that room. Over time, after the arrival of a second daughter, the nook became the kids' playroom.

Virginia Woolf may have extolled the virtues of having a room of one's own, but we parents can't even stake our claim for a little kitchen nook. Some may be fortunate to have a home office like I have. But an office is a place where you work, not where you dream, relax, plan, express yourself, and simply be.

When my own kids were younger, I decided I wanted a personal spot in my home, a tree house of sorts where I could do a deep relaxation or meditate or even read without interruption after I pulled the up ladder. Since we didn't have an extra room, I decided to appropriate a walk-in closet. Its cocoon-like atmosphere made me feel supported and secure.

Of course, there were challenges in trying to transform that closet. For one, it had hanging clothes. I found if I pushed the items forward there was extra space in the back. Since shelves ran up that back wall, I cleared the bottom rung of some old boots and mittens and laid down a colorful scarf, turning it into a joint altar/reading table. I placed my favorite books and some spiritual artifacts on the shelf and added a small meditation cushion on the floor nearby. My space was ready.

The next night after my kids fell asleep I went into the closet and closed the door. I first performed a dedication ceremony I'd found online. This involved honoring the four elements: Burning sage to cleanse the air (mercifully, it also got rid of the smell of feet), flicking water from a small bowl to honor life, placing a rock in each corner for grounding, and illuminating a small candle for light. I then sat on my cushion and meditated for a few minutes, followed by reading a few pages of a lovely book. I emerged maybe 20 minutes after entering, but for how soothed I felt it could have been hours.

When I told my friend Anne about my new sacred space, she peppered me with questions. She didn't have room in her closet. Could her place be a favorite club chair? I didn't see why not, as long as she made sure her kids understood that this was mom's special furniture and they couldn't climb on her lap when she was there. Anne refrained from paying bills or watching TV in that chair, using it mostly for deep breathing exercises, spiritual reading, or savoring a piece of her beloved artisan chocolate. Soon she could feel her brain detox the minute her butt hit the cushy pillows.

I myself got much use out of my closet nook. I liked just knowing that it was there, beckoning me to its comfy space even if at that moment I was dealing with a kid's skinned knee or hurt feelings and couldn't enter. When I did go in, mostly in the evening after the kids were asleep and just before I was, I barely remembered I was in a closet.

Which brings me to my observation that a sacred space doesn't actually have to be a space at all. If you can't rustle up any part of your home or patio to call your own, you can invent a sacred space in your mind. Simply close your eyes and envision yourself any place you feel peaceful, be it a beach, forest, or that crawl space under the house you grew up in. Be specific, recalling the smells, sounds, textures, and colors. Then "sit" in your space as often as you can. For as Woolf also noted in *A Room of One's Own*, "There is no gate, no lock, no bolt that you can set upon the freedom of my mind."

Nourish Yourself

Call an Old Friend

One day an image of my old college roommate sprang into my mind. Back in school, we'd spent many late nights sharing plans, dreams, and insights about careers, men, our bodies, life, and love. Debbie taught me the rules of baseball; I taught her the history of American feminism. Together, we explored shows, movies, concerts, and cooking. My favorite college memory, in fact, was the evening she and I tried to poach the whole fish our roommates had purchased, rather than the fillets we were expecting. We laughed hysterically as we struggled to decapitate and debone the creature until we thought to call an expert—her mother. Guffaws continued as we futilely tried to follow her mom's over-the-phone instructions until eventually we tossed the whole mess into the trash and ordered pizza.

Surprisingly (or maybe not; I believe that when you focus on something the universe helps line it up for you), Debbie called me a few days later, even though we hadn't spoken in years. I was thrilled for the opportunity to relive our memories and to share our current plans, dreams, and insights about careers, men, our bodies, life, love, and now also children.

I think new friends are incredibly valuable. When you have children, these tend to be the parents of kids in your son or daughter's classroom or after-school programs, or those you bond with while your respective kids play in the park. But I believe that old friends who have a recurring role in our personal drama rather than the one-shot cameos the newer ones may have add something special to our lives. As author Cheryl Strayed writes in *Tiny Beautiful Things*, "The healing power of even the most microscopic exchange with someone who knows in a flash precisely what you're talking about because she experienced that thing too cannot be overestimated."

Reminiscing with an old friend gives shape to the overgrown jungle that is our past. Friends who've been there when times may have been tough for you understand where you're coming from in a way newer ones can never grasp. They also highlight the ways we have changed. As a child, for example, I was overly eager to please. As one of my oldest friends confirmed years later, I always wanted to be the teacher's pet. Hearing that from this woman reminded me as an adult to keep an eye out for this tendency, because now I prefer to stay closer to my own desires.

But busy parents easily let old friends slide off of our horizon. We hardly have time to shower—when are we going to pick up the phone and chat with a long-lost pal? Still, it's important to carve out space for things that feed us, and the support that friendship brings makes it one of the most vital foods. Fortunately, social media and smartphones have made keeping in touch easier. You can resurrect a languishing friendship by messaging or emailing someone at a late-night hour when you can't call. If your old buddy isn't too far away and has kids of her own, you might get everyone together rather than try to find adult-only time. Even texting a photo of your family to a forgotten friend can rekindle the old alliance.

When Debbie and I reconnected, I remembered right away why I'd always liked her. Debbie is a soft terry robe, the friend who wraps herself around you without artifice or judgment. She said just the right things to make me feel good, even after I'd shared a story that involved a behavior of which I wasn't proud. Debbie's down-to-earth mien reminds me to keep my focus on what's important in my life (family, friends, joyful activities, writing) and not to get sidetracked by wild chases down trails that might be important to others but that don't excite me. I'm glad to have her back in my life.

Perhaps you left a once-meaningful friendship on a not-so-high note. An argument over a romantic partner, maybe, or about missing her special party. If you valued the bond before that, it may be worth calling the friend with a mea culpa (even if it wasn't actually your fault). It's possible she won't absolve you at first, but that doesn't mean you shouldn't attempt it. As the insightful Cheryl Strayed also reminds us, "Forgiveness doesn't sit there like a pretty boy in a bar. Forgiveness is the old fat guy you have to haul up a hill." When you get to the top, though, even if you had to work hard to get there, the view can be worth it.

Of course, not all of the friends from our past should be dragged into our present. I regularly get Facebook requests from people I'd rather leave in my history. Letting go of unsatisfying or even destructive relationships is also a way of taking care of yourself.

But for those old pals you value, give yourself the gift of their presence in your current life. Then, when your kids get older and you finally have time for a lingering meal or even a whole weekend away together, you'll have already cultivated the connection that's deep and lasting and true.

Nourish Yourself

Expose Yourself to Positive Images

I've never watched a Wes Craven film. Never read Bret Easton Ellis (or even Stieg Larsson, for that matter). Violent or suspenseful media might be called "thrillers," but for me the thrill comes from staying away.

Most parents have deep convictions about not wanting their "vulnerable" little ones exposed to negative imagery. We ban them from watching certain movies, playing teen-rated video games, or reading specific books. But we often don't realize that we are vulnerable too. Our mind is equally affected by what we see and hear. I remember being struck by the disconnect as I chatted with a woman at a park who proudly declared that she prohibited her child from seeing a violent film, all the while clutching her dog-eared copy of the classic horror book *Carrie*.

I learned my lesson one Sunday night years ago when my kids were asleep, my husband was out with a friend, and I had a rare evening with nothing to do. I flipped around for a movie to watch on TV and found one some friends had praised as clever and smart. Just a few minutes in, however, someone was murdered—with blood and guts exploding onto the walls and floor. (This from a "clever and smart" film!) By the time I got in bed that night, my heart was pounding so hard I thought it might split open. I couldn't sleep for hours. When I awoke the next morning, the image of that gore was still front and center, like a bad tune you can't get out of your head. The late Kundalini yoga master Yogi Bhajan used to say he didn't understand why spiritual seekers would eat healthy food, avoid smoking, and raise their Kundalini energy through movement, but debase their minds by watching trashy movies. After that night I had to agree.

I'm not saying you should never read a well-written thriller or watch a great movie that has some gratuitous violence. I recently got hooked on the AMC historical drama *Turn: Washington's Spies*, and the Revolutionary War battles were pretty graphic. But I'm careful what I feed my brain. When the violence comes on the TV, I look away, and when unpleasant images pop up in a book I'm otherwise enjoying, I skim those pages.

I'm clear that what we choose to focus on sets the tone for everything we experience after. There's an adage that says when you walk down the street, one side has rose bushes, the other dog poop, and you get to choose which way you look. The dog poop—that is, the exciting, the violent, the suspenseful media—may be more compelling, at least to a mind conditioned for action. But the roses yield the greater reward, in the form of peaceful thoughts and the ability to carry that calm through the rest of your day.

"Think only on good things, and righteous. Dwell not in negativity and darkness," spiritual author Neale Donald Walsch writes in *Conversations With God, Book 3*. And when it's put like that you can't help wondering why we would choose all that unnecessary darkness. I think it's because we don't see violent entertainment as the mind pollution it is.

When my friends used to tell me they'd read a great book or seen a terrific movie, I'd put those items on my list without asking for details. Only after a few times when I was sitting in the theater or cracking open the novel did I realize everyone clearly has his own definition of "terrific." And terrific for me—and maybe for you—now has to mean not only done well, but also in keeping with my desire to stay uplifted.

Here's what I wished I'd done that Sunday evening years ago: Read any of the spiritual books or lighthearted novels that always line my nightstand, listened to soothing music, or found a streaming PG-rated movie (or even one rated R for sex, not violence). I believe filling the mind with positive imagery is especially important at night, because our thoughts before we drift off to sleep influence the mindset we wake up to.

Although films, books, TV news, and other media are the prime way we expose ourselves to unnecessary poisons, they aren't the only ways. If you want to treat your mind as carefully as you do your body—or even as you do your hair, clothing, house, or car—you might commit to being selective about everything you absorb. Although I acknowledge the suffering that happened during the Holocaust, for example, I won't go to any Holocaust museums because I don't see the need to sear my mind with the horrifying details. I'd rather spend the day in a park, or even in a hospital where at least the suffering is borne by people I can help by being there. Try being picky about what you mentally take in for one week and see if it makes a difference.

"I do not at all understand the mystery of grace—only that it meets us where we are but does not leave us where it found us," writes author Anne Lamott. To give that grace a chance to enter, I believe we need to set a positive scene. Don't only ask your child to avoid the bloody and violent images that in our culture they are so easily exposed to. Honor that ideal for yourself, too.

Nourish Yourself

Follow Your Passions

At a friend's weekly card game, one of the mothers tried to impose a rule that no one should talk about their child or spouse. "I told her if I followed that edict I'd have absolutely nothing to say," my friend later confided in me, embarrassed by her realization.

Of course parents feel passionately about our children. We follow their every word, every move, every mood with delight. I am as swept up in this as anyone. I can still tell you the order in which my son's baby teeth erupted (he's an adult now), and I admit I'd be thrilled to do this if I thought you might be the least bit interested. Get a couple of new parents in a room and they can pass hours conferring over breastfeeding moments and bowel movements. Parents of older kids as easily share tales of sports and academic prowess or moments when their child treated another with love.

But what my friend understood that day is that we also have other passions, which too easily get overlooked in the family fog. Her passions included painting, politics, and pointy shoes—dozens of which once lined her closet before she traded shoe-shopping expeditions for jaunts to the toy store. Another friend adores baking. Other pals enjoy sailing, playing piano, hiking in the wilderness, and sharing their math skills with disadvantaged kids. I love yoga and sitting on the beach as the sun sets over the water. But because our kids were little at the time, none of us had done these things in ages.

Maybe we feel we're not entitled to indulge these passions, a phrase that itself has selfish connotations. We tell ourselves we'll be able to do them when our kids are older (and as someone with older kids, I can confirm that's true). But passion is important in all the stages of life. It's the fire that powers our internal furnace—or, as Neale Donald Walsch writes in *Conversation with God, Book 2*, "Passion is God wanting to say 'hi.'"

We postpone our fervor at our peril. People who are depressed, for example, have largely lost touch with their passions. Some experts believe that passion must be expressed frequently or it can erupt uncontrollably, like lava trying to be held down in the earth. In the most extreme cases repressed passion is what causes someone to abandon his or her kids to search for inner answers, like Meryl Streep's character in the 1979 classic, *Kramer vs. Kramer*. When you go to bed at night feeling like you haven't accomplished anything—even though you did a million chores and maybe also worked a paying job—it's because you didn't spend time honoring what excites you.

To follow our passions, we first must get in touch with them. I used to look askance at people's hungers that didn't coincide with mine. Women spending hours at the gym lifting massive weights. Kim Kardashian's huge selection of handbags and shoes, which require a separate closet. People playing (or listening to) country music. Now I realize that that diversity is what makes the world interesting. Any activity that generates intense emotion is right for you.

If you don't know what you thirst for, think back to your youth and reflect on what made your heart beat faster then. Did you love racing your bike at top speed, the wind whooshing through your hair? Treasure collecting coins, stamps, shells, or figurines? Performing African or Middle Eastern dances? If those recollections still bring on a smile, why not give them—or something akin to them—another go? Be open to noticing activities that inspire you as you hear of them, or glance through Meetup notices for something to try.

Ideally, you'll be able to integrate your family into a least some of your passions. You can ride your bike solo early on Saturday morning, for instance, but also go out during the week with your little one in an attached seat or with an older child riding alongside. I shifted my passion for collecting from matchbook covers of places I'd been (which I had to give up anyway when restaurants and stores stopped offering matches) to quarters with the states on them, which I could do with my kids. When I remembered how much I liked puzzles in my childhood, I began buying the 500-piece pictures that appealed to me, and even though it was hard for them my kids would try to lend a hand.

Ask yourself which of your passions you've stopped enjoying since you became a parent. Then, don't aim to merely "indulge" that interest—cherish your passion as the daily path to enlightenment it is.

Nourish Yourself

Create!

My preschool-aged daughter was decorating Popsicle sticks one day, eagerly pulling the flat wooden rods from a jam-packed box and decorating each with colors of her choosing. I sat for a while, silently admiring her focus and joy, until she finally asked, "Why don't you make some pretty sticks, too, mom?" I realized I hadn't even considered taking one. You see, I have this image of myself: I am not artistic.

This belief, pounded into my head over many years by art teachers, well-meaning friends, and the arts community, stopped me from comfortably doing anything related to design. I'd buy flowers already put into a pretty arrangement by the store, bring desserts to social occasions from an artisan bakery so as to guarantee they'd be attractive, and avoid those women's-night-out craft parties at all cost.

I know I'm not alone in having viewed painterly pursuits as the purview of talented artists, singing for those with a pleasant voice, or dancing full-out in public for trained ballerinas. (Funny, though,

I've always encouraged everyone to write, rather than thinking it should be reserved only for people who make their living at it like I do.) As parents, we know that our kids love to do these activities and more. One of my most treasured memories is my son as a toddler loudly belting Elvis' "You ain't nothing but a hound dog," as he swirled around the living room, not caring a whit that he was completely out of tune. Most of us believe kids do this only because they're too young to recognize their lack of talent. (Sadly, no matter how hard we try to protect them, someone will eventually clue them in.)

Creativity is not necessarily the same as passion, although they can be linked (See "Follow Your Passions"). Passion is following our interest in something we get joy from, but that can be something other people create, like collecting art or watching a ballet. Creativity always comes from inside. It is letting our soul out to express itself in the physical world. In some ways, I consider creating the closest I can get to Source—even more than meditating. When I'm writing an essay or novel or even a Facebook post, I feel Source flowing through me. What's more, this experience is similar to the way the universe was created: First there is "nothing" and then, via my computer (or paintbrush, baking supplies, my moving body…) it miraculously transforms into a "thing."

When we allow the belief that we're not good enough to shut down our creativity in any arena, we deprive ourselves of many moments of joy. There was a great magazine article about a woman whose husband whipped out his tuba and loudly honked away during every dinner party the couple hosted. At first, the wife was mortified by his lack of musicality. Eventually, though, she saw the thrill her husband derived from playing, regardless of the fact—of which he was fully aware—that Julliard would never come calling.

He didn't fuss about how well he played; he simply treasured the fun of putting his lips to the mouthpiece and blowing.

Most of us resist being so joyfully oblivious. But in a way, that's what is required to create, because in our culture judging someone's creation—whether that's a professional writer's novel or your Aunt Mae's noodle pudding—is practically in our genes. Everyone always asks, "What did you think of that?" when we leave a performance or a pastime. In order to free ourselves to create, we have to teach ourselves to stop caring what they think. We also must stop caring what *we* think. As Elizabeth Gilbert, author of *Big Magic,* observes, "Fear is always triggered by creativity, because creativity asks you to enter into realms of uncertain outcome, and fear hates uncertain outcome. This is nothing to be ashamed of."

One way to get past this fear is to view creation as a process rather than an outcome, a detour instead of a destination—even if someplace is arrived at in the end. I was able to create my first novel only because I focused on making up individual sentences and scenes, rather than the book that was materializing from that. Had I entertained the thought, never far from the surface, that I wasn't talented or experienced enough to write a book, I would have been sunk. Like the tuba-tooting husband, we must emphasize the moving rather than the choreographed dance; the manipulation of clay under our fingers rather than the resulting bowl; or the swirl of beautiful colors from each stroke, not the painting you'll wind up with.

I once knew some swamis who held a weekly art class where they drew and painted on old newspapers. They didn't care how it turned out because at the end of the evening it all went into the recycling bin. Similarly, my favorite preschool, Sunflower Creative Arts (where both my kids went), focuses on the process involved in making art, like melting wax over paper or painting with a brush in each hand. The kids treasure their output, but largely because it reflects the thrill they had in the doing. I love that the writer Anne Lamott (who's got plenty of talent) labels her initial attempts "shitty first draft," thus freeing herself to stop the self-judgment as the words pour forth.

The day with the Popsicle sticks convinced me there was no reason to hold myself back any longer. I selected some sticks and set to work—or, rather, to play. I got such pleasure from marking up the tiny wooden canvases that when my daughter moved on to her next activity, I kept at it. Then I admired, not so much my handiwork, but the fact that I'd allowed myself to participate. I placed both our finished products on our family altar, to remind myself to thaw my creative juices from their freeze-dried worry jar more often and let them flow.

The next time I took my kids to the plaster painting studio I selected my own piece. As my children worked away, this time so did I. And when I went to a rare holiday evening out without my kids, I joined all the women around the piano to sing carols. (I admit it was tough not to judge myself there, because before puberty turned my singing voice to mush I'd had a beautiful alto.) I won't say I've become perfectly uninhibited: I wouldn't sing a solo in public—nor play a tuba!—and I still buy my flowers already arranged in the vase. But I'm much less likely to stop myself from expressing creatively for fear it's not good.

Anne Lamott warns of the tragedy of finding yourself at the end of your life having always squashed your creative impulses. "What if you wake up some day, and you're 65, or 75, and you… were just so strung out on perfectionism and people-pleasing that you forgot to have a big juicy creative life…. It's going to break your heart. Don't let this happen."

While your kids are young you may not have the time—or the mental bandwidth—to write your magnum opus (or paint a big mural, enter a baking competition…). But it's tough to expect your creativity to go from zero to 60 once they get older. You have to nurture the seeds over time.

Start with small things now. Paint and dance and make music with your child. Allow yourself to cook or bake with a little extra flair. Write a few pages in a journal before bed. Buy colorful crepe papers and decorate a birthday package yourself. As your kids mature, let your creations do so, also. Then, when you reach Lamott's mythical old age, you'll more likely have had that big juicy creative life–along with a full and happy heart.

"Everything is unfolding perfectly...

and as you relax and find ease,
in your attitude of trust, knowing that
well-being is your birthright,
amazing things will happen."
—Esther "Abraham" Hicks

Acknowledgments

It's hard to know whom to thank for a book that has been written over two decades' time. I started this book years ago, when my kids were small. Several people read chapters and commented on the book's potential in its early stages. I especially appreciate the encouragement at that time of Joe Durepos, Aimee Anderson, and Ed Keller.

After a while, I put the manuscript away, deciding I needed the perspective on parenting that comes when you're not in the thick of the cacophony, crayons, and carpools. After dusting off my draft last year, I've been further blessed to have had additional readers, including Susan Caruso and Lisa Erickson, as well as the wise people who offered their comments on several chapters I published on the *Huffington Post*.

A book about parenting has many influencers. There were the insightful moms and dads in the spiritual parenting discussion group we formed when our kids were babies, the members of my local La Leche League, and the wonderful people in the years' long Tuesday night spiritual discussion group I participated in. The parents I got to know, befriend, and be enlightened by at my children's Family Time mommy and me program, Sunflower Creative Arts preschool, and Claremont Montessori elementary school in South Florida gave me much food for thought. The beloved teachers at those places taught me a lot about honoring and trusting my heart and my child, especially Karen Deerwester, Susan Caruso, Shelly

Zachs, Harvey and Nancy Hallenberg, Linda Walley, Terry Ellis, James Estarellas, Bonnie Striker, and others.

Of course, there were my spiritual teachers. Those who contributed in person to my upliftment include the heartfelt Swamis Satchidananda, Ashokananda, Ramananda, and Jyotirmayananda; the loving Rabbis Phillip and Shoni Labowitz and Marc Labowitz; and the fabulous Reverends Barbara Lunde and Jill Guerra. I've also grown tremendously by reading the works of and/or attending retreats with the numerous spiritual thinkers I have cited in this book.

Finally, I have to thank my amazing family for helping to make me who I am today: my fantastic parents and sisters; my wonderful mother-, brothers- and sister-in-law; and, most especially, my much-adored husband, Gary, and two kids.

I hope this book inspires you in your own spiritual evolution, and helps you acknowledge all the beautiful souls who have and will continue to help you keep soaring.

About the author

Meryl Davids Landau is the author of the spiritual women's novel *Downward Dog, Upward Fog*, named a fiction book of the year finalist in the small-press competition by *Foreword Reviews,* which called it "an inspirational gem." Meryl's articles on parenting, spirituality, and health have been published in numerous outlets, including *Parents, O: The Oprah Magazine, Glamour, Redbook, Reader's Digest, Self, Yoga Journal,* and *Huffington Post.* Her magazine articles have won numerous awards, including a first-place award by the American Society of Journalists and Authors, and a nomination for a prestigious National Magazine Award. Meryl lives with her husband in South Florida, and is the mother of two children, now young adults.

www.ingramcontent.com/pod-product-compliance
Lightning Source LLC
Chambersburg PA
CBHW051822040426
42447CB00006B/319